Dropshipping With Shopify

The Ultimate Guide to Start Your Online Business. Learn Proven Strategies to Avoid Common Mistakes, Choose the Right Suppliers and the Best Products to Maximize Your Profits.

Philip Hayes

ISBN: 978-1-914358-42-5

This document is geared towards providing exact and reliable information in regards to the topic and issue covered. The publication is sold with the idea that the publisher is not required to render accounting, officially permitted, or otherwise, qualified services. If advice is necessary, legal or professional, a practiced individual in the profession should be ordered.

- From a Declaration of Principles which was accepted and approved equally by a Committee of the American Bar Association and a Committee of Publishers and Associations.

The information provided herein is stated to be truthful and consistent, in that any liability, in terms of inattention or otherwise, by any usage or abuse of any policies, processes, or directions contained within is the solitary and utter responsibility of the recipient reader.

Table of Contents

Introduction:

It has never been simpler to earn money online. For along the era, on building up a web page, web names and hosting, purchasing and holding large sums of stock and all the bother to fill and deliver the shipments, you must have had to pay a huge amount of money. By removing the stress and the hard work off your side and getting the cash coming into your savings to account instantly, the invention of dropshipping keeps track of all that.

Dropshipping is a type of distribution that allows customers to buy goods from a producer, wholesaler, or another retailer separately and forward them to your consumer.

This ensures that you might increase the efficiency and get it delivered straight to your consumer from either the supplier's warehouses instead of delivering products to your customers in a conventional manner, where you would buy stocks and send that from your supplier to your customer.

In brief, dropshipping gives you a chance to become a "mediator," a chance to market to the consumer without necessarily hanging on to any stock whatever. The costs are far lower; locating the vendors, advertising the products, and delivering the shipments to the retailer is all you have to do. They give you the gap in between the expense of their item as well as the price at which they offer, helping you to comfortably make money for the least amount of risk and effort.

Dropshipping by no means a modern scheme; well before the Internet was invented, it was in operation over one manner or the other. The net also made things so clearer, simpler and brought up additional consumers to the market.

You've got the right idea if you'd like to learn more about dropshipping and how much you can quickly make rewards.

For several decades, Shopify has become a massively successful framework, allowing people to launch their own online stores without learning a tone of complex technological items.

The issue would be that not everybody has the resources for their site to spend early on products; that's one of the key factors that frightened people off the online store.

Luckily, despite needing to pay a single cent upfront on stocks for it, anyone can begin and operate their private Shopify store. What? How? Shopify. Right.

Dropshipping makes it possible without the need for a high initial cost to supply a supermarket, and it also seems to have a range of several other advantages.

Remember that there are a few disadvantages to dropshipping, which would also be covered in this guide. But there are a few strategies to minimize such pitfalls, and you're going to hear about several of them, too.

When you're about to know how to build money from your own store while wasting a penny on products, you'll like to review this document back and forth.

Let's start off.

Chapter 1: What is Dropshipping:

Allow me to share with you a short description for those of you who might not understand what dropshipping is.

Dropshipping is a means for people or firms to market goods without holding any stock by directly delivering products from the manufacturers or a reseller to consumers.

Let's assume you would like to open a business providing pet products, but you do not have product resources, nor do you choose to deal with yourselves with the hassle and expense of holding stocks and shipping items. So you email a drop shipping firm, get a list of your items, and link it to the website at Shopify.

When a consumer orders an order with your store, by placing orders with both the drop shipper and making it delivered straight to the consumers, you literally place the order. You have never had to contact the object at all since it's shipped straight from either the warehouse to the consumer.

Unless you can locate a reputable dropshipping business, this functions perfectly, so what you want to do is serve with the go by arranging the transaction and sending it to the client. Firstly, the strategy is based on you, and then to buy the items, you use the money they gave you.

To get started, you don't get to have much cash at all, except paying with your domain and the charge for Shopify. Win-win it is!

1.1 How does dropshipping at Shopify work:

Dropshipping is a practice by which you market goods to the consumer as a manufacturer while necessarily hanging on to either inventory or commodity. You send the order straight to your preferred seller when you sell a commodity; you receive the product, accept the invoice, and then send back the gap between both the product fee you produce and the cost you charge. You never get to see the thing, you never see it, and you wouldn't require any fees to be managed or processed.

Although the transactions do not have to be managed, a few companies will encourage you to handle your payments and some that will require you to deal with your own shipping company. Even then, using these solutions avoids the aim of opting to operate the organization utilizing dropshipping.

There are indeed distinctions between a normal e-commerce company and the main business using the dropshipping company model.

Gross margins, operational logistics, operational costs, profit velocity, and entry barriers are among the variations. Below, we will discuss each one of the variations separately.

- **Operating Margins**: The gross income is the formula used to calculate the price policy and operational effectiveness of a business. And that's the calculation of the percentage of the business's income, which is left over for accounting for adjustable manufacturing costs. For a business utilizing dropshipping, the profit margin would often be smaller than a traditional e-commerce company, so you do not have the responsibility of carrying inventory or merchandise delivery.

- **Operational Logistics**: You do not need to hold any inventory or transport any items if you are operating a company utilizing drop shipping, which allows you to operate the shop from practically anywhere around the world. You have to understand the logistics of operating a store, restocking the stock, and organizing delivery while operating a traditional e-commerce shop.

- **Operational costs**: You must recognize the expense of paying for your warehouse, charging for the workers to operate your storage facility, paying for the stock, delivery and managing customer care if you are operating a conventional e-commerce enterprise. In contrast, the expense of operating a corporation utilizing the dropshipping system is restricted to taking orders and delivering them to a wholesaler or retailer only for customer care.

- **Profit Velocity**: While dropshipping is amazingly hands-off, from an operating point of view, keeping stocks is a far easier means of ramping up profitability. That's because when you get the opportunity to purchase goods in bulk with an international source and market it at a cheaper discount, the profit margins are even higher.

- **Entry barriers**: Entry barriers involve the presence of high beginning costs and other challenges prohibiting the entrance of a new player into a market. A business utilizing dropshipping is simpler to clone and set up than a company that holds its product and exports it.

Case in the World Today

Let's say you're choosing to sell guitars. You will need to purchase in actual stock for a typical retailer to purchase and store 25 guitars.

And you'd have to locate clients who would like to buy guitars.

Let's assume you're selling three guitars, and then the profits fell off. You're quitting the corporation and winding up with a room with a bunch of guitars you can't market and no funds in your financial institution. Life will be better with drop-shipping:

- To sell instruments, you created a website with an online shop.

- You're offering a $350 "Silver Shadow" guitar.

- You receive a response from your online shop for one Silver Shadow.

- The request is submitted to the producer or retailer of your distributor. The of those you have picked

- And for Silver Shadow, they bill you $200 plus $10 for them all to send. It goes straight to the client,

- The manufacturer is planning on bringing the order and sends the Silver Shadow to your Purchaser.

- You make 90 dollars on the deal,

- Repeat to see the income rise as fast as you want to.

In certain situations, the orders are handled by the retailer, and the gap between your price and theirs, minus any delivery charges, will be sent to you.

While there are numerous benefits of opting to create and operate a conventional e-commerce company instead of building a cleaning store, there are considerably fewer risks involved with utilizing dropshipping.

The start-up costs are often much smaller; there are fewer uncertainties, ensuring you can start earning profits from your company quicker than you could ever from a commonly managed eCommerce shop. Therefore, an organization that utilizes drop shipping is less expensive and needs less attention to resources than operating a warehouse and holding stock, at least before the full-time work is taken over (and becomes your sole source of income). If you don't make some profits for any reason or make substantially more sales than you expected, there is also no you didn't purchase or run out with a common commodity with difficulties with keeping the stock; these concerns lie and are your supplier's fault. You always choose to depend on a rear supplier if the supplier sells out of a component.

1.2 Shopify is a great platform for Dropshipping:

We take a peek at a hot issue for vendors at present, Shopify dropshipping, in today's scenario.

If there's one aspect many of us have lately gone thru, it's the reality of operating from home! For several, because of COVID-19 limitations and prolonged lockout duration, this has occurred mostly by mistake.

What it has most definitely achieved for certain individuals has offered them stability, different talents in managing time and a task balance that we may not have enjoyed before.

There is no question that when lockout continues to relax and potential directions are determined, there is likely to be a lot of 're-thinking' taking on. There would be a powerful urge to take a new path and enjoy the versatility of working at home!

Start an e-commerce company is expected to be an enticing prospect for those with it in mind.

It's a fresh start, delivering the desired work-life balance, promoting quality time and keeping food mostly on the table. What isn't there to like? And choices are available: eBay, Amazon, Etsy or Shopify.

A dropshipping company is a common alternative right now for Shopify. There is no inventory to stock, no parcels to send, enabling you to focus on selling your goods, making profits and concentrating on expanding your company with your precious time and resources. It sounds terrific. But, it isn't a silver bullet or a simple scheme to get wealthy.

Overnight, you can't demand a full bank account, but it's an interesting option to explore simply as a part-time company. So, whether you are preparing to start an e-commerce venture, why do you choose the famous dropshipping model of Shopify?

So, then you're au-fait with both the dropshipping concept and Shopify. What's so amazing about the pair that they fit well together? Well, with very little trouble, a Shopify store could be created, not only because it interfaces with the dropshipping system so seamlessly.

Dropshipping with Shopify is a perfect choice if you're not using the money to handle development, delivery and distribution, which is one of the easiest and most common tools you can use to build and operate your business.

- **Dropshipper friendly:** Shopify massively embraces the dropshipping concept, and thus there are several applications specially created for dropshipping that fit perfectly with the framework. When launching your company, this certainly makes things simpler for you. Oberlo, for instance, is a dropshipping program that actually deals with Shopify.

- **The host of design features:** Shopify provides a broad variety of features that allows users to build an e-commerce company instead of just a site, so it's great for newcomers! To develop the shop and have all the designs in order, the online retailer creator is for you. Along with other fantastic features that make managing the orders, ads and payments super easy, you can select a range of free and premium design models.

- **Simple to use:** Among the most browser platforms accessible is the Shopify platform. It's easy and not overwhelming, even if its functionality and features are abundant. The videos are simple to follow, as they do a nice job of clarifying how to do the app, and you may have several customers so that you can quickly recruit more teammates as the shop expands and that you need more support.

- **Not require you to overthink:** It's as basic as getting an understanding of the goods you want to market and combining your ideas with a dropshipping solution to get underway. Shopify offers all the resources you have to begin offering and get established.

1.3   The Right Mindset:

Are you already doing dropshipping work but unsure whether you have the right mindset to open your shop? If so, then this book is going to be wonderful for you! We're going to go through six points you should remember, so you can get your store started the best way.

You may master dropshipping concepts for free of cost:

First of all, most individuals assume that to excel in dropshipping, they need a professional dropshipping program. The great news is, this isn't real. Out there, there are fantastic courses, don't buy a course because it guarantees you a certain profit. Buy a course since, for instance, you want to read all about Facebook Advertising.

Learn when to end dropshipping:

See, the beauty of dropshipping is, until you can sell them in the online shop, you don't have to buy hundreds or even thousands of the same items.

One by one, you will acquire them. This ensures that anytime anyone makes an order at your online shop, you pay for items! Isn't that lovely? You will discover a great thing: you can sell the stuff before agreeing to a big bulk order. You need to note here right now that you need to realize when to avoid dropshipping.

If your product performs well and you realize you have reached a Niche to offer your product to, then purchasing your product in bulk is great. So if it's not going to sell well, avoid buying instantly.

You don't have to buy a premade shop:

Assume you are contemplating launching a new dropshipping project. In that scenario, from one of the several websites selling them, you might have come across the idea of purchasing a premade dropshipping shop. As a novice, purchasing those shops is not necessary.

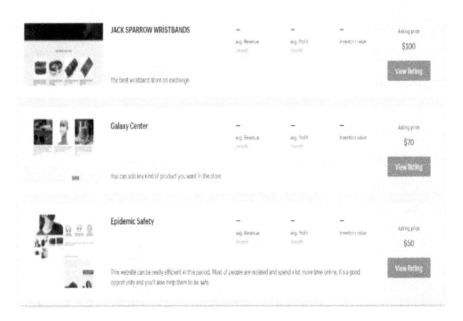

Be distinctive, not like the majority:

"You may be thinking right now, "Huh, but I'm dropshipping. My shop should look like many other dropshipping shops. 'There are too many individuals studying about dropshipping and launching dropshipping shops. For starters, type 'Dropshipping' in Google Trends:

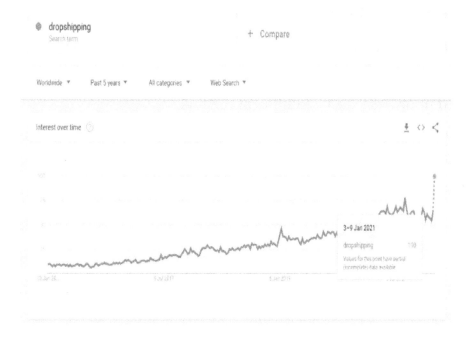

See just how big the dropshipping industry is?

Everyone wants a slice of it because it was marketed by too many of these "geniuses" as a simple way to make money digitally. But are you sure of what the saddest part is? Most of them don't bring their dropshipping store into any effort. They open their shop without altering things, purchase some items and begin advertisement.

This ensures that many dropshipping individuals market the same goods from the same data they obtained from maybe even the same dropshipping distributors. Getting the same commodity, of course, is not a negative thing. But it would certainly not benefit you in the long term to have the same pictures, explanations, style, and so on as well!

Dropshipping is only a strategy for fulfillment:

Until beginning with dropshipping, there is another excellent thing you should remember. Now the process you use to deliver your orders is just a fulfillment method.

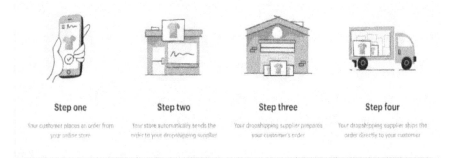

How does dropshipping work?

No more up front inventory costs or shipping logistics. With dropshipping, products are sent directly from your wholesaler to your customers.

Step one	Step two	Step three	Step four
Your customer places an order from your online store	Your store automatically sends the order to your dropshipping supplier	Your dropshipping supplier prepares your customer's order	Your dropshipping supplier ships the order directly to your customer

There are three primary types of e-commerce fulfillment:

- **Dropshipping:** Your dropshipping provider will do all for you for this delivery strategy. (Manufacturing of products, distribution, storage, etc.)

- **Third-party satisfaction (or 3PL):** From obtaining the stock from your retailer to storing returning items, this firm can do anything for you.

- **Fulfillment of in-house order:** You hold the inventory in your home, for instance, and submit instructions from there as well.

Don't trust anything online that you see:

Thanks to too many 'high-number of' YouTube video clips oriented towards dropshipping, people have very high hopes. "Now people think something such as "dropshipping is equivalent to making billions easily" or "dropshipping is equivalent to quick money. But that is not at all real. Dropshipping is a real company you're launching, and it always relies on a few variables to raise cash from it.

1.4   Oberlo

Oberlo is a website that makes it simple to locate things to sell digitally. You will browse a range of different items like appliances, games, and makeup with Oberlo. Oberlo lets you locate goods and connect them to your very own online shop from vendors all around the planet.

Once a deal has been made, the retailer delivers the goods straight to your client from their store. Your goods don't need to be packed, processed, or delivered.

To promote your goods in your online shop, on social networks, and across online markets, you could use Oberlo. If you're still using AliExpress dropshipping, you can add your current items to your Oberlo profile.

Once you have purchased goods, set your prices and set up a delivery plan, it follows a similar protocol with each order to bring products to your customers:

1. Through your Shopify store, a client places an order and pays the price you have chosen.

2. You get a bill notification from your payment processor.

3. At the selling cost, you buy the commodity.

4. Your provider directly delivers the order to your client.

5. They collect their order from your client.

1.5 Pros and Cons of Dropshipping:

Comparing the dropshipping approach to the conventional e-commerce store already has demonstrated a few of the advantages and drawbacks of using dropshipping for a company. We will weigh the pros and cons below, as they relate directly to an organization utilizing dropshipping.

Dropshipping has a range of pros and cons that and before you try to get interested in the company, and you have to consider these.

Understanding the following benefits and drawbacks will guarantee you, and your organization makes the right decision and will guarantee that you are not shocked by any of the items you experience when you set up and start your firm.

- **Pros:**

- **Less Capital**: Undoubtedly, that's the single greatest benefit in dropshipping. With no need to provide huge sums of money to spend thousands of dollars upfront in stock, anyone can open its e-commerce shop. Dropshipping removes that obstacle by requiring an individual to have money locked up in stock. Once the deal is completed for dropshipping and the buyer charges the cash, there is no need to make any orders. This enables you to launch your own e-commerce company with little cash in hand today. In reality, you can also use those sites to build your e-commerce company provided for free. While these alternatives are generally not as effective as the other channels, it is a way to make a little capital to build a good business model.

- **Easy to Get Going**: It has not been easier to operate your own e-commerce company, especially since you no longer have to manage physical products. You don't need to think anymore when you pick dropshipping:

✓ Rental or ownership of space for warehouses

- ✓ Loading orders and distribution of them

- ✓ Monitor your accounting inventory

- ✓ Managing things returned

- ✓ Inbound shipments handling

- ✓ Having to order items to maintain your rate of inventory

- **Low Overheads:** The lack of necessity for you all to rent or purchase storage room or buy in stock holds your costs to a low. Many individuals use more than just a desktop or laptop with overhead costs of less than $100 per month to operate their dropshipping company by their own homes. These overhead costs will rise as the company expands, but they will still be smaller than running a brick & click business or perhaps an online business where you require physical stock.

- **Flexibility in Location**: As long as you link to the internet, dropshipping can be performed almost anywhere. Communicating with your clients and your vendors is all you need to be willing to do, and it ensures you can operate your organization from everywhere.

- **Good Product Selection**: You will offer your prospective buyers a really large selection of products to pick from because there is no requirement to buy stock upfront. If your preferred suppliers store an object, you can place it for selling on your site with no added expenses associated. This suggests that you will manage to keep it available for sale while eating up precious storage space if you find a certain commodity is seldom bought. It also offers the ability to introduce a fresh idea to the consumer even without danger that it may not take off. This is very profitable if you want to market specific goods and products which are focused on current phenomena, such as TV shows or movies.

- Easy Scaling: The degree of business you earn when you operate a typical company is directly linked to the number of effort you put in. Almost all of the extra work associated with order processing is borne by them by utilizing dropshipping services, which helps you expand the company with less pressure and inconvenience of the additional effort included. More sales often bring further jobs, particularly in customer support, but utilizing dropshipping enables you to grow the job than a conventional organization better.

While further requests would be equal to additional customer support demands, because you will not be liable for handling and shipping the inquiries, you would be able to provide a strong customer support model. A strong model of customer care is important. And if you charge a bit more than a brick-and-mortar store, as soon as it reaches they are respected as clients, customers would be able to compensate for the comfort of shopping at home.

Even if they are newcomers or long-established, these advantages translate to that of an appealing model for all retailers. However, it isn't all roses; although it can be versatile and comfortable, it does arrive at a charge.

- **Cons:**

- **Low Margins**: That's the biggest downside to dropshipping, especially if you are operating in a really specific society. Since dropshipping is too simple to get moving and the rates are minimal, ever more individuals open an office and offer at the lowest available rates to try and then get the money in. Such individuals spend nothing in launching an organization to continue to operate with the lowest of margins.

These merchants probably provide very low-quality websites with virtually non-existent customer care in certain situations but do not deter prospective buyers from evaluating rates. They would opt for the lowest, more frequently than not. Your profitability will quite quickly vanish due to the growth of competition. Picking a place that is ideally adapted to dropshipping is the only way to get around this.

- **Issues with Inventory**: It is reasonably straightforward to monitor which products are in stock, limited and out of stock while you have a company where you hold your own inventory. However, you focus on other vendors as you want to dropship, and all these suppliers not only provide your clients, they also operate with other retailers. Thus, the levels of inventory shift regularly. You may use technology that would allow you to synchronize your inventory levels to that of your suppliers. However, this does not often work really well, and certain suppliers would not provide the required technology. This will add to a really disappointing experience for the consumers because they believe they will be eligible to pay a commodity only to find out that it would be currently unavailable, and they may have to wait a long time for an item they already have paid for, or wait for such a refund also to be processed until they can buy from some other merchant.

- **Issues with Shipping:** Many dropshippers deal for multiple separate suppliers, so this ensures that many drop shippers supply the goods you deliver. For the shipping expenses, this model will create problems. E.g., let's say that three separate items have been purchased from you by a consumer. These come from various vendors, ensuring that three types of shipping costs are charged, one per piece. It is not smart to move on such prices to the clients since they would conclude that you will be overcharging for delivery, but it is not possible to simplify the cost estimates, even though you want to do it. The easiest way to do it is to aggregate the expense of delivery through vendors, some of whom you're going to make certain cash from, some you're going to have to spend on.

When they buy three items from one retailer and all three products are delivered to them separately, this may often contribute to consumers becoming irritated. It also allows it more challenging for clients to believe like as they monitor their shipments and have three separate reference numbers, they need power. The enhanced uncertainty that may occur if a consumer is attempting to get assistance with one thing but has messed up the overall numbers or index futures is another possible concern.

- **Issues with Suppliers:** Another danger where things will go bad is to operate an online company that uses vendors to drop the clients. There will be occasions when you and the dropshipping vendors are not even on the same page, including technological problems to misunderstanding.

  How many occasions have you ever had to excuse yourself for anything which was not your mistake? From time - to - time, the top dropshipping providers can make mistakes, so it is up to you to accept accountability for their failures and apologize. If you choose low-quality vendors, you can carry on more hassle than you could ever handle, with products lost from packages mixed up with the bad quality packaging. They might not have been your negligence, and it may suffer from your brand and organization.

When operating a company of vendors doing dropshipping, one other factor to bear in mind is that so many online stores deal with even more than one provider of goods. Because there is no universal specification for data types, things may quickly get confusing. This ensures everything will be unique from one provider to the other from order management, account configuration, and billing. If you switch the specifics from one manufacturer to the next, this may lead to complex and costly partnerships with the vendors. When selecting the vendors, it's something to hold in mind.

A short note: dropshipping is something you do as store's owner, while the retailer that supplies, bundles, and delivers the items you offer is a dropshipper.

1.6   Basic inquiries regarding dropshipping:

There may be issues with dropshipping, but that's true with every organization you can conceive about. Fortunately, it's pretty easy to cope with any of these concerns.

- **Shipping Errors:**

When the dropshipping business mess up, one of the more popular concerns that can occur is. They may forget to ship your purchase request rapidly, or they may deliver the wrong object.

When this occurs, taking the blame, apologizing to the client, and attempting to make things right is crucial. For starters, you could give their new order a discount or include a free gift for both the consumer. You may also give the postage charge to be refunded or give cheap expedited shipping for the substitute order.

Yes, this could lead you to make less gain on the deal. This might also make you risk a profit on the offer. But note, this was not the responsibility of the client. Ultimately, when you choose the specific dropshipping company, it's indeed your duty.

You can certainly make sure that the drop shipper pays to correct the mistake, such as giving the customer a specific change if the incorrect item was shipped, but with any updates you owe the customer, you're likely with your own.

Because the one you prefer appears to have trouble quite much, be able to turn to a new provider. For this purpose, if you need to switch fast, it's a good idea to locate multiple vendors before you even open your shop. If one runs out of a single commodity, it is often a smart practice to utilize several vendors so that another firm will seamlessly take up the slack.

- **Inventory Issues:**

A possible concern is resource control. To control their products, certain vendors will use firms such as Ordoro or eCommHub, enabling you to coordinate your stock with theirs, although not every organization uses either of these.

Find organizations with an order tracking platform whenever necessary, which will quickly help you synchronize the inventory. This won't eradicate inventory shortages, but it will improve.

➢ http://www.ordoro.com

➢ http://www.ecommhub.com

- **Fraud:**

From time - to - time, you may have to contend with fake orders, but if you approve PayPal, they can normally manage that form of scam for you. When you order an item and have evidence of shipping, if the buyer wants to get their cash back, you'll be covered by their Vendor Security Scheme. When clients use a credit card and pay, they will have a machine that scans for misuse. If you assume theft, send a call to a consumer or contact them.

In order to check you have the right one, are polite and courteous, and remind them that you are calling to check their request and delivery confirmation.

You can recommend canceling their order and offering a reimbursement if you cannot reach the consumer within a good length of time. If the consumer contacts you just after the cancellation of their order, clarify that you tried to call them to check their order and that their reach address didn't seem to work. Sorry, please remind them they will be able to position their orders again.

Please make sure to provide tracking records on each shipment so that you can show that it has been shipped. Only because you can't confirm the item was shipped you wouldn't want to owe someone an opportunity to get their money back for legal sales.

1.7   How dropshippers make a profit:

The discrepancy between how much the buyer pays for the goods versus how much the item costs you to purchase from the retailer is your net profit. The following factors influence your gross margins:

- The sorts of things you want to market

- The price that you set for your goods

- Your Plan for Shipment

Chapter 2: The Supply Chain & Fulfillment Process:

We spoke a bit about how dropshipping functions, and before you decide whether you want to do it for your business, there seem to be a few additional things you should know on how the process operates.

The dropshipping supply chain includes three participants that you need to talk about:

2.1 Manufacturers:

They generate the goods but typically do not market to the customer directly. Certain unusual suppliers may sell dropshipping, but usually, they would go thru a wholesaler first.

2.2 Wholesalers:

By serving as an intermediary, they promote the selling process. They purchase from the maker at the lowest amount and then market to consumers at a small discount. They could provide dropshipping options.

2.3 Retailers:

Retailers purchase from wholesalers or even producers. The market, usually at very high markups, to the consumer. They can use dropshipping as the source of the commodity as well.

Any of these may potentially be a drop shipper, although it is more likely to be offered through wholesalers. At the vendor stage, the greatest source for dropshipping will be that you'll get the highest rates, but most producers realize it without all the problems of dropshipping, they will easily sell their goods to wholesalers, so it's not simple to find manufacturers that can dropship.

You may still locate dealers that will drop shipping, but you would have to spend more than they do to make a profit; at much higher rates, you won't be finding too many customers.

Many dropshippers would be fairly opaque to the user. They would typically send the goods on your behalf, sometimes with your logos and return addresses on the box, so it looks like the item was delivered to the consumer by your corporation.

You will have to contend with the eventual return, of course, and in that, in this situation, you will merely work with the drop shipper to make any necessary adjustments.

Chapter 3: How Dropshipping works:

Two of the best general dropshipping tactics on Shopify would be looking for a distributor in North America (NOAM) or elsewhere on the planet, utilizing supplier servers, or finding a kind of Shopify application that links you or your shop with various vendors.

We recommend Oberlo for the final, Shopify's stage that rents different business holders catch goods to offer. Using Oberlo, by pressing a key, you may hunt AliExpress and ingress the things that spark your devotion straight to Oberlo, which is connected to your amazing Shopify shop.

When a person purchases an item, the Oberlo application will enable you to fulfill their demand. Oberlo happily optimizes this process. As the shop owner, all you need to ensure is that your data is correct and click the "'order'" icon. The commodity is then sent directly to the customer from the dropshipping provider of AliExpress, anywhere on the globe they might exist.

3.1 How to excel in the dropshipping business:

Take the six measures below if you are ready to launch a company that will contend with supermarket giants and does it with a small budget. Although starting a drop shipping company does not need a lot of beginning capital, it would require a massive amount of hard work.

Conduct competition analysis:

Know, other drop delivery activities and supermarket companies, including Amazon and Wal-Mart, can contend with your business. This is exactly where many prospective dropshippers journey go bad when hunting for a product with slight to not at all rivalry. That's an indication that there's little shop for that exact thing.

There are numerous explanations why a product, like high delivery prices, supplier and production difficulties or low-profit limits, does not have many opportunities. As it indicates a strong market and the market model is viable, search for a rivalry.

Optimize and evaluate:

To build your business, you have to monitor all of the accessible performance metrics. This entails traffic from Google Analytics and pixel data for Facebook migration if it is the key consumer acquisition platform. If you can monitor every single transition recognize where the buyer comes from and what route they followed on the page that finally lead to a sale—it helps you scale up what works and remove what doesn't.

Establish a plan for consumer growth:

It's good to have a wonderful brand plus a webpage, but you don't have a market without customers demanding to purchase it. There are a lot of avenues to draw new buyers, but launching a Facebook advertisement promotion is the utmost effective choice.

This aids you exact from the outset to produce revenues and salary, which will lead to fast climbing. FB (Facebook) helps you to place the offer in front of strongly focused spectators nonstop. This offers you the potential to contend straight with the main labels and shops.

You will have to contemplate the long run, so the stress can also be on selecting search engine marketing and online advertising. Collect emails from the outset and set up automatic series of emails providing deals and promotional offers. Without extra ads and publicity expenses, it's a simple way to exploit the current client base and raise sales.

Develop a platform for eCommerce:

The easiest way to start a website that promotes an economic model for dropshipping is to utilize a basic e-commerce application such as Shopify. To get ready to launch, you wouldn't require a tech history, and it has loads of applications to help boost revenue.

It's a far wiser step to use one of the plug-and-play solutions, particularly in the early cycle, even though you have a massive budget that would enable you to build a customized solution employing a web design and development firm. When you are formed, and the money comes in, further website functionality may be discussed.

Secure a vendor:

A new partnership with the poor supplier will destroy your company, so this move mustn't be hurried. Keep a close watch properly. Most drop shipping vendors are based overseas, rendering contact highly necessary, both in terms of efficiency of reply and the ability to comprehend each other. If you are not 100 percent secure of a prospective supplier's contact skills, pass forward and begin the quest.

In order to locate and connect with prospective producers and vendors, Alibaba has become one of the biggest online assets. In the case that the company expands rapidly, be sure you ask a lot of questions to understand what their manufacturing capacities are. You want to make confident that for you, they have the capacity to scale.

Pick your niche:

The niche you choose must be laser-focused but something that you are truly involved in. It would be hard to sell a product line that isn't centred. You would be more likely to be frustrated if you are not excited about the niche you choose since it takes a lot of effort to scale a dropshipping enterprise effectively. When choosing your niche, below are several things to consider:

Offer anything local that isn't readily accessible. Choose something down the street that the client can't reach. You become more appealing to a prospective buyer that way.

Build a brand of your own:

If you can repackage whatever it is you are promoting and sign it off as one of your own products, your drop shipping company would have more credibility. Look for a product or range that you can white mark and market with custom packaging and labeling as your own company.

Making sure customers are looking for the commodity aggressively.

To review any popular search words relating to your future niche, use Google's Keyword Planner and Patterns. If no one is looking for what you are working on the offer, you are sunk in the ocean before you even launch.

Be sure that the commodity appeals to quick discretionary income consumers. You want to enjoy the real potential retention rate while you are focusing on driving traffic to your website, so most users would never return. Impulse sales can be caused by the goods you offer and draw others with the monetary capacity to create a buy on the place.

It is really necessary to have low shipping costs. And if the retailer or producer will do the delivery, it will serve as a consumer repellant if the cost is too high. Find one that is affordable to send, as this often offers you the opportunity to offer your buyers free delivery and bear the expenditure as a business expense to gain further purchases.

Strive for attractive gains:

Your emphasis is on promotion and consumer retention while you are operating a drop shipping business model because the amount of effort needed to sell a $20 item is basically the same as selling a $1,500 item. Choose a niche for goods with better costs.

3.2 Techniques for moving traffic to your Shopify shop:

It is an amazing achievement to start a new e-commerce company on Shopify. However, even with quality goods, your sales can lose steam. You may want to poke around your organic traffic if that's the situation. It can very well be that the traffic on the website is poor.

The fewer clients that you get, the fewer sales you make, after all.

If this is valid for online merchants with the highest results, then smaller companies on Shopify will need to try to get customers to their site aggressively.

The more visitors you receive, the more revenue you make, so your profits will automatically rise with the visitors, even though the poor baseline conversion rate remains true. However, don't fret. There are a few tried and tested forms of generating traffic from organic websites and eventually improving revenue.

Having your websites next to them is the secret to getting your future clients to your online store. If it's through social networking sites or through web pages, the more visibility you can receive for your website will help improve your e-commerce site traffic. Here are some popular ways to improve your organic web traffic and, more specifically, raise your revenue.

3.3 Enhance your Shopify store for the Web Search Traffic:

They would typically do a little bit of homework on their preferred search engines until your prospective clients realize that your company or store operates. Google AdWords offers a common and reliable approach to access your relevant traffic since it helps you specifically put your website at the front of the searchers' hands.

But if you're not involved in pay-per-click ads and would like to have your website next to your target group without costing a penny, you may do so through search engine optimization.

The method of rendering your online store more accessible to the search engines is search engine optimization (SEO).

There are several approaches to do this, most of which start by recognizing what the target group is looking for.

Key phrases are the searching keywords that users use with web pages and can help you in the enhancement of your search engine.

More significantly, if you recognize what your customer is looking for, then you will build the right content for your online store to draw them.

When a collection of useful keywords that are important to both your product and your niche market has been compiled, start utilizing them all over your website.

The best positions where keywords can be found are:

- Titles of commodity
- Descriptions of commodity
- Alt Marks on Photos
- Any More Material

Attracting consumers using content marketing:

Much like your product names, any other material on your website can help draw traffic to your Shopify website. The material you add doesn't need to be overly detailed, either. It will do the trick with a quick section at the bottom of each login screen.

Write Visitor Articles for other sites inside your niche:

Another significant part of the SEO e-commerce marketing campaign that shop owners often overlook is that search engines prefer websites with a healthy backlink profile. This suggests that there are potentially a number of other domains linked to the websites on the top of search engine results lists.

The more ties that point to your page, the stronger connection you have.

Your title tag will grow when you gain more connections to your website.

Basically, your domain authority is a virtual scorecard that tells search engines like Google that your website is recommended by other users on the internet so you might expect, the more reviews you provide by connections, the higher the search engines can rate your website. The search engines are informed through a comprehensive connection profile that your platform is a reliable source of useful knowledge. The more you rate, the faster it is possible to improve website traffic.

But how can you get your favorite connection from other sites?

It is best to propose to write a guest post for many other blogs inside your niche instead of waiting for other websites to guide traffic to you via a connection.

You may begin by exploring your favorite blogs within your niche to see if they welcome guest bloggers. Talk out when they do, and see if you should compose a guest blog article.

If you would like a broader scope, then you should look inside your niche for every blog that welcomes guest authors. You can do this by using Google's Site: Operator.

Using the Site: User lets you find possibilities for guest blog entries. Try typing 'in title: writing for us + your specialty' to use this feature. For e.g., if your Shopify shop sells items in the fitness sector, then inside that niche area, you would want to write guest blogging for blogs.

In this case, type 'in title to use the function: write for us + wellness's to create a list of guest blogging possibilities within the wellbeing niche.

Go out to as many forums as you can afford and plan to write a few regular guest blog entries. Have a reference back to your Shopify store in your author profile, typically at the bottom of the blog article. You can steadily build your connection account and your organic search along with it by using it.

Write Blog Post Highlights of your business contacts:

Creating a blog post that highlights influencers in your target industry is another way to get more connections and boost traffic to your online shop.

Conduct a little bit of homework to find out in your niche which the big players are. These persons also referred to as "influencers," are sure to have your target audience's interest and can be a big source of referral traffic. In an expert round-up type blog article, compose a brief feature on each of them until you have your list of popular blogs.

Please share it on social media after the article is written and tag each one of the blogs. You could also reach out by email to the blog owners and let everyone know that you've just published a feature on them.

While not all of them can react to your content or post it, some of them could. Some may share the role on their social networking accounts, and others will refer to their own blog posts with the message.

Use Social Network Influencer Marketing:

And as the target market's popular bloggers help you boost page views, so do social networking, too. The fastest way to bring your product or shop via social media in front of your target group is by launching a publicity campaign with influencers. An influencer on social media is any profile that has a large number of reasonably active fans.

Influencer marketing not only raises brand visibility and site traffic, but the total order value on Shopify often increases. Collaborating with an influencer on social media earns substantial benefits and is well justified the commitment.

Incorporate Social Networking:

It would help if you made confident that you are able to accept all of the latest traffic on social media now that you have run the advertising and influencer plan. This is why it is necessary to combine your favorite social networking channels with your Shopify store.

Instagram is highly important as it has the second-largest acquisition cost, after Polyvore, above all other social network marketing tactics.

In other terms, as a consequence of Instagram marketing, people spent more than almost any other form of social media advertising.

Shopify and Instagram have officially collaborated to make things simpler than ever to shop on Instagram. Instagram also has "shoppable posts" that allow users to tap the picture icon to get product information.

The consumer can purchase the product right in the Shopify store by clicking on the product details.

By linking your Instagram page to your online store you make the buying process as simple as possible for your target audience.

Facebook also remains firm as the outlet for the bulk of revenue, even if Instagram has the second-highest order quantity of all social network marketing. So combining your Facebook company page with your

Shopify store is a smart idea, as well.

You make it much simpler for consumers to communicate with your Shopify store by turning your company page into a

Facebook store without ever needing to adjust their virtual everyday behaviors. The quicker it is for prospective buyers to enter your shop, the more traffic you'll receive.

Chapter 4: Finding and Working With Suppliers:

This can be tricky to pick a supplier for the dropshipping company, but it can enable you to realize that there's various suppliers who have been at it for several years. Some lead the industry in broad industries, and this may be the perfect way to start in your new company since the goods you offer are already recognized and have gained appreciation from the market. You could have to trade off and then work in restricted ways with your profitability, and you will need to be careful in reviewing the terms of the contract of each corporation, but every one of these can create a backdoor into that you can start a profitable long-term business.

Not all drop shippers are made equally, or to guarantee that your organization is effective, you like to ensure you chose the best provider. There are a few items that your provider wants to provide and some things that are less essential but can have better accessibility.

Any of the items you'll be searching at in a provider include:

✓ Can the retailer have trained elected officials?

✓ Can the supplier commit with them a single individual committed towards your acct;

✓ They are skilled in becoming technologically sophisticated;

✓ Why can you register your bookings?

- ✓ Where they are situated:

- ✓ They're an integrated organization.

- ✓ How soon can they deliver their shipments?

- ✓ Why can they hold you within that know on backorders and products outside from stock?

- ✓ How fast can they send you their tracking details and purchase order?

- ✓ What payment types do they approve? And what payment options do they endorse?

- ✓ What type of rates are they charging?

Once you start searching for a supplier, locating the supplier may seem challenging. Credible enterprises to distinguish them from illegal businesses. There are a few tricks to choosing a decent provider for dropshipping.

One crucial point to bear in mind when you start approaching suppliers would be that they may well be the secret to selecting the best supplier, even though they are not the right match for you. Please ensure you always ask every supplier you meet if they can guide you in the correct direction to approach a supplier that best meets your needs. Since they are in the business, they are sure to have connections that will help you and are typically prepared to share the details.

Looking at social media is yet another way you could improve the chances of having a reliable supplier to deal with. Often, through a family member, neighbor, or colleague who might be in the field or meet someone in the field, you may find a path. Any path is a successful path, even though it contributes to a dead end.

4.1 Common Suppliers:

In suppliers, there are several options that you will deal with. Bearing in mind that we'd like to have an organized provider, have the technology to support them, and are loyal to what they're doing, you would want to begin with a supplier that's already made a reputation for itself and the goods they offer, as appeared differently concerning a supplier and commodity that is not as well established to the common society.

Here are four of the choices that are best:

- **Shopify:**

Today, Shopify is among the leading internet e-commerce platforms and has portions of its website devoted only to dropshipping. Shopify provides the option of creating an account and a dropshipping shop, and they will also help you build a decent hosting and domain name, all of which ensure that you will be fully operational in much less than 30 minutes. Amazon and eBay are two of the major suppliers that you can connect to via Shopify, enabling you to sell their goods on your site. Now you can select your suppliers.

Shopify introduces a platform for e-commerce that is exclusive to them, and they often provide a broad variety of payment choices. This ensures that the broader the variety of payment choices, the greater potential you have of getting in clients, you will move those choices on to your clients. Shopify has been known for a long time and delivers a comprehensive package, helping you to comfortably and efficiently get your organization fully operational.

It's quick to get going, just go to their website and select between paid and free hosting. If you'd like to start with the free one, you may upgrade later. Then complete guidance on how to build your website and get going will be provided to you. Optionally, since it is hosted anywhere else, you will use items from their platform with your own page. This makes it possible for you to receive funds from your clients and meet all of the legal provisions that involve data protection and personal details.

For Amazon a merchant, Shopify is among the favorite choices, is among the simplest to use, and runs incredibly well. This can be tailored quite fully to fit you or to encourage you to build a really unique shop. To summarize, Shopify helps you to conform to the preferences, stopping you from appearing just the same for all the other online stores out there.

Even though they have done most of the work and analysis for you, this is a good foundation for developing your company. It is a good bet to choose either Amazon or eBay as your dropshipper for your organization since both have been operating for a long time and have also developed their own identities and public image.

- **Private Label:**

You must concentrate on creating a reputation before you launch your company, one that would be recognized and valued, and a private label benefits either you or the retailer or distributor you select. Almost the first move with your organization is to import the goods you choose to market, goods that do not crack easily which have comfort for the customer.

The second and perhaps most significant move are to make your brand known to current and future clients. The more customers remember your brand, the higher it is possible that your revenue rate will be. You may help this along by selecting producers or suppliers who will submit your goods via Private Label. This operates by encouraging the consumer to position their shipment with you, thus delivering that to the retailer and directly dispatching the goods to the consumer.

The returning name and address would be that of the company in most situations, but for Private Label, this will be yours. This ensures that whether they have some concerns or queries, the consumer would assume that the item has arrived from you, and they'll only contact you. This helps you to create a brand reputation, but using trustworthy vendors, depends on you, and you deliver top-quality customer support.

In general, manufacturers are really willing to use the sale of private labels since it suggests that they are often not interested in any consumer problems.

To sum up, while you are looking to get your brand out and develop a company without casting doubt on Amazon or eBay's popularity, a private label makes perfect sense. It will require a bit extra time to select a supplier since you must do the job yourself and would like to guarantee that you perform for the right supplier. However, you'll still gain a better profit when you accept ownership for the client support and are ready to bargain the supplier's rates.

- **Amazon FBA:**

Amazon is a big household brand, and for someone who develops or operates a company that is not founded, the FBA is their answer. It provides you the chance to use the outstanding prestige of Amazon as either a background for the organization without needing to compensate for it.

Regrettably, it is not a really meant program for dropshippers, so you ought to be willing to transfer actual goods to an Amazon distribution center when such an order arrives in Amazon and utilize their shipping options, which fulfills the shipment for you. Even so, about any inventory, you should not have to shell out for warehouse room as Amazon can hold that one for you, and also working with the packaging and shipping-they cost a tiny amount for this.

To sum up, Amazon FBA would not be the first option for an organization that requires Dropshipper. Even so, whether you have found a suitable wholesale provider that does not dropship but gives a good price on the commodity, it may be a good option. This might be a realistic choice for your organization if you choose to reap those rates' benefits without needing to spend in a factory and workers for doing your delivery to you.

- **Retail Arbitrage:**

This is yet another approach, and it is not dropshipping completely. Retail arbitrage is just about discovering decent goods you can turn around and sell at a benefit at the correct amount. This means that you require money, and you will need to be associated with a successful organization for distribution. That's a better addition for Amazon FBA to use, and it saves you both room and time. At the best price, the key is to find the right goods and that you can be using dropshipping wholesalers.

Pick very wisely the correct items and not be hesitant to try tiny. In relation to market arbitrage, dropshipping will operate really well, and you will see the huge profits start pouring in.

4.2   Building Your Supply Chain:

Unlike with a conventional company, Dropshipping does not enable you to build and manage a supply chain. It does need you, though, to cultivate your suppliers and subcontractors. Your retailer is the individual liable for determining the rates, conditions of payment, dates of delivery, and also assessing if an object is eligible at all. A reliable way to really get favorable rates, fair conditions, and wider demand is to establish a good partnership with your provider.

To strengthen the partnership you have had with your provider, there are a few items you should do:

- To pay on time to develop trust and become a valued client;

- If they request an estimation of the goods you plan to sell in a specified period, set simple and realistic goals;

- Notice that they will have other clients, and they're not exclusively yours;

- When you put instructions to expedite the operation, learn whatever they need from you;

- Whenever there is an accident, don't accuse the leader, instead, collaborate with them just to find a solution;

- Knowing somebody on a personal level seems to render them more likely to help you out, being buddies with your executive; and

- Train them to appreciate whatever you need, such as fresh photos of the product and Notifications on improvements to goods, products out of stock and withdrawn Commodities.

4.3   Finding the Right Suppliers and Working with Them:

One critical aspect you have to do until you continue the right suppliers' quest is to know how to say the difference between a true wholesale supplier and a department store that works like one. The manufacturer orders their products from a genuine wholesaler and delivers far higher deals than a supermarket would.

4.4   How to Spot a Fake Dropshipping Wholesaler:

You would most definitely come along with a variety of bogus ones during your quest for a wholesaler. Unfortunately, in ads, many of the individual wholesalers are really not that successful and, as being such, maybe even tougher to locate. This suggests that rather than the true ones, the false ones would appear in the queries. To assess whether a wholesaler is legitimate or not, use the following techniques:

- **Ongoing Fees:**

To buy from them, a true wholesaler would not cost you a monthly subscription. This is most possibly a bogus wholesaler unless you are called for a monthly service or subscription charge.

Make confident you're not staring at a list of vendors. There are folders with wholesaler lists, ordered and evaluated by business or commodity category to assure they are valid. They can charge rates, whether it's a one-off or a monthly fee, for obtaining the records.

- **Selling to the Public:**

You ought to register for a wholesale acct if you really want genuine wholesaler rates because that tends to mean you have to show that you are operating a legitimate company and will have to stand in line for clearance until you can put an order. If the wholesaler supplies the general public with wholesale rates, they really aren't real; they are retailers selling goods at heavily inflated costs.

You can come across legal wholesale fees, such as:

✓ **Per-Order**: A dropshipping cost per shipment, from $2 to $5 or even more, is paid by certain legal dropshippers. This would rely on the order's scope and scale. As packaging and delivering orders placed is more costly than transporting consignments, this is an industry norm.

✓ **Minimum Order Size**: For an initial batch, certain wholesalers may provide a minimum price, which is the very lowest percentage that you would purchase for the first attempt. This would be to sort out among the real customers the window-shoppers. This can trigger no end of problems for dropshippers-assume lets the wholesaler had the first shipment of at least $500, and the shipments just average about $150. Just because then you can access your dropshipping accounts, there would be little point in wasting $500 on one thing, then what do you do? The simplest method is to clarify the condition's wholesaler and give as a credit line towards orders to pre-pay $500 upfront. This helps you to achieve the minimum cost necessary, and a huge order would not need to be imposed.

4.5   Finding a Wholesale Supplier:

Now you learn how you would launch your quest to say a fake from a true wholesaler for the right supplier. There are several different techniques, and you'll have to pick the ones that fit well for you:

- **Contact the Manufacturer:**

That's the best means of locating a legitimate wholesaler ever, though. If you recognize which thing you would like to see, just contact the manufacturer to tell them whether they're in stock. And inquire about the wholesale distributors' lists. Then, and seeing how they enable dropshipping and if you open an account with them, you should settle down and contact each one.

- **Use Google to Search:**

This would seem to be a fairly obvious path, but bear in mind a couple of things:

- ✓ In marketing, wholesalers really aren't healthy, so the quest must be thorough. Until you discover what you might be searching for, you just have to muddle through dozens of data. More likely than not, once you are finished, you would not be able to locate any valid results for your quest. Via the first ten or so pages of findings of the quest.

- ✓ They still may not provide quite up-to-date websites but do not evaluate them. A badly built, out-of-date website would not actually suggest that they should not give you lots of reliable services.

- ✓ As wholesalers do not prefer to use SEO widely, you may have to use modifications in your search words. Add "reseller", "distributor", "warehouse", "bulk" and "supplier" not only check for wholesalers.

Be able to invest time on it and couldn't just hop in the hunt for the first answer or two.

- **Place Your Order with the Competition:**

Order from the competition if you find it challenging to select the correct source. Find a retailer that appears like a dropship and put a tiny shipment with them. Search the tracking number on Google when you get the shipment, and you can find out the initial shipper's name. Mail them immediately then.

4.6   Before you Contact the Suppliers:

You have the supplier list and are ready to begin. You ought to get it in place before you do:

- You have to be legitimate, and you have to be willing to give facts evidence you are running a legal organization. To guarantee that the organization is lawfully established first, several wholesalers can just inform licensed consumers what their actual price is.

- It's important to consider how you look to a wholesaler. They seem to be those who pretend to get the next brilliant concept and marketing proposal regularly approach them and are barraged with queries before vanishing from the face of the planet. Because of that and, several vendors are not going to be very focused on supporting you. Don't bind up their people before making a sale by posing lots of questions or requesting discounts; what you'll gain is a poor name, and they're not going to continue to negotiate with you.

- Contact the retailer by picking up the machine. Not everyone should be done with it, and most vendors are still more than willing to support you via text. If a definitive business proposal is delivered and you can persuade everyone, you are real.

4.7   How to Find a Good Supplier:

As just regarding everything, each supplier, especially when it comes to dropshipping, is different. The strongest vendors can illustrate any or more of these six characteristics:

- **Industry Focus and Expert Staff:**

The best vendors can hire sales managers who are experienced, who understand the market well and the goods being offered. You need a representative who understands what they're talking about to be able to call you back.

- **Dedicated Support Staff:**

A sales manager will be allocated to you by high-performing dropshipper suppliers; the agent will take care of you and will assist you with any complaints or concerns you might have. If you don't get a committed agent, you'll notice it takes much longer to fix questions, and you'll have to keep calling want your answers. Finding a committed leader it is the same one you deal with would also make it easy for you to develop a more intimate partnership with the agent that would support you as well.

- **Fully Invested in Technology:**

There are also successful suppliers who have bad websites

that are obsolete, but a very good supplier would realize and spend on technology's advantages. They can give you lots of services such as real-time product monitoring, a detailed online collection, customizable data charges, and order web history.

- **Use Email for Orders:**

This does not seem like something very big, but that can be time-intensive to have to ring up any request since it could be placed on the online platform. Using emails to approve instructions dramatically accelerates the process.

- **Located Centrally:**

It is safer for you to select a drop shipper that is somewhat centrally placed if you reside in a wide nation, just like the USA. This ensures that much of the orders will be shipped to your clients during a few business days. It will take in a week or so for the shipments to find their way around the nation if the supplier is situated on a coast that can pay much more delivery costs.

- **Properly Organized and Efficient:**

You can come along with vendors who recruit extremely efficient workers and have strong processes that offer you the largely error-free service. Others would get the other command mixed up. The main issue is that even with using them, you will not assess their competence, and therefore it is better to put a short test order for any of the preferred vendors, tedious as it might be. This teaches you more about how they act, and you can figure out:

✓ How each business performs the order phase

✓ How fast they ship the orders out

✓ How fast they supply you with details and receipts for monitoring

✓ When the order has been shipped, the package content

4.8   Payment Options:

Often producers would recognize compensation in either of those two ways:

- **Credit Cards:**

They would most definitely ask you to utilize a big credit card to pay for the order while you are starting your trip with a provider. You may always find that it truly is the best choice until your organization is formed.

- **Net Terms:**

Another popular approach is to use net invoice words. This indicates that to compensate the provider, you only have a fixed amount of days. Net 30 terminologies imply that with all bought products, you had 30 days to compensate.

Most lenders would require collateral checks until they authorize you to do this since, in effect, they are lending you money. This is normal; if you're questioned for any comparisons, don't be put off.

An essential aspect of the company is going to make sure you deal with the best provider. As a business, the bad supplier will seriously impede your development and can decide that you're not really effective. You believe the provider to guarantee that the product is right and comes to your consumer the manner it was shipped, and then you never have seen the product. The last step you need to do is wind up with a bogus supplier or a supplier with the instructions you give to them, which won't carry through. This would leave you with less cash with a poor name among your clients. You are even less likely to pick a bogus supplier if you make sure that you will be vigilant about your choice of supplier and so don't sign up for the first one you came across, and you can set yourself up to succeed.

You can start on the process of discovering the supplier that would suit you or your business strategy, now that you know how to access a real supplier and how to recognize and avoid a fraudulent supplier. When you have located a seller who can do the dropshipping for you, you will be ready to place your clients' orders.

Chapter 5: Choosing the Best Products:

Choosing the best market as well as the right goods to spend your efforts on is the greatest challenge you would have to conquer. This judgment is vital to the success or failure of your dropshipping company. The only main failure you're going to make is selecting a product based on your own desires or personal preferences, particularly if you'd like to create a genuinely profitable dropshipping company; you have to provide what the other peoples want, not what you really want. Particularly if you are not the type of individual to adopt patterns and are these type of individual that is sometimes called "outside of the box." I can't even tell you which product to offer, but I can offer tips about how to pick the correct ones.

5.1   How to Choose the Right Product:

Your organization will have an ongoing climb to become profitable without a strong product portfolio. It may seem impossible to try to find what it is you're trying to market, with potentially millions of items out there. The item you chose will also pose other concerns that you might have to work on. For starters, shipping could become an issue if you are going to sell refrigerators. Depending on where your clients work, whether you are selling alcohol, there could be regulatory limits.

Market analysis can sound daunting, but knowing the products can cater to the audience you will reach through your site is important. You should monitor the industry dynamics if you're using an understanding of what you intend to do to see how well the commodity performs on the market. If you're not sure what you'd like to offer, you will always find consumer patterns helpful. Business dynamics will indicate what items consumers are purchasing or are interested in buying at the moment.

Hunt for items that address a question that your target group has. Find a fresh and improved product to sell if the customer is fed current with the newest product range. Choosing a commodity that is not readily obtainable nearby or a national brand that is sought by a region outside of where it is actually accessible may also is a brilliant choice. Another recommendation is to select a commodity-focused on the target audience's desires. This may be in the shape of a new TV show that is beginning or a new style.

It often applies to aiming for a difference in chances. When you want a commodity that several other rivals are now offering, try something that you're doing differently or more than anyone else. This may be an upgraded product element, a segment that your rivals totally ignore or perhaps something about your marketing campaign.

Since you are trying to market a commodity-based with something that is popular at the moment, ensuring that you capitalize early upon on pattern, there appear to become more individuals who purchase the commodity at the outset of a trend. Someone else is already moved on to another item if you step on the bandwagon either at the end of the pattern. Do not hesitate too long to leverage on development in the industry because you believe you are trying to restart a fading trend.

When you make your decisions, it is necessary to take into account product profitability. It would take a lot of time and resources on a product range that varies year after year to guarantee that the product selection is held up-to-date and does not include last year's choices, which could no matter how long be eligible. A reduced churn product would enable you to put money into a much more informative website that'll be applicable for a longer span of time.

Don't be frightened of looking at smaller segments and niches of products. While there could be fewer prospective buyers, there may still be less rivalry, making it easy to even get to the top of the search results and often more cost-effective in the form of ads. The right product is an important aspect of your growth, take your time and don't jump for the first good-looking product.

To create a good organization, you need to be able to do all of the following:

5.2 How Access to Exclusive Distribution or Pricing:

Being ready to bargain unique product deals and the exclusive prices would offer you the advantage without any need to import or produce your own item to sell online. These aren't really quick items to arrange, and you can notice that you're really out-priced, and at wholesale rates, some dropshippers would still offer the same or equivalent.

You have to come up with a way to persuade the buyers that the commodity you offer is of higher quality than for the competition, whether you can have exclusive distribution, particularly if the rivalry sells knock-off products at lower prices. That's where the website "about us" page becomes much more useful, although it is a great way to gather the fact that you are unique to the product.

5.3 Sell at the Lowest Possible Price:

You will cheat if you might be willing to sell your goods at the lowest cost, Consumers from a reasonably wide chunk of the niche segment. The main thing is that since you actually won't be able to appreciate the gain, you are destined to struggle.

The cheap cost is not often the primary motivating factor behind the choice of a consumer to shop. Customers seem to choose to invest their cash on the best benefit and lowest cost of a commodity. This suggests that you ought to persuade them that perhaps the best decision is to invest a little extra cash in your goods although there is less downside and more appeal to them.

5.4   Add Your Value Outside of the Price:

Consider in terms of having data that fits the items selected. A real capitalist can fix challenges while at the same time offering goods at high rates. In your unique niche, ensure to give suggestions and knowledgeable recommendations. Your customer support is one extremely efficient way to bring value to the goods outside of the costs. If you are willing to address all the queries of your consumer without needing to call you but are able to reply to any emails easily, your web store would stick out from the rest.

Price Adding:

This is not always simple, and for certain niches, it will fit easier than that of others. Look for main features that make it simple to add content value, specifically in niches that:

5.5   Have Several Components:

Potential consumers are more inclined to search for details on the internet, whether they consist of many separate components. If you order a new chair for the workplace, for instance, it's an easy investment. On the other side, if you wanted to purchase a full protection device for home monitoring, you would like to understand how each aspect of the system functions and how everything works together.

The further modules and the greater range that these elements can bring, the stronger the chance to building up the reputation by delivering product knowledge and education.

You have a fantastic opportunity to create an interactive platform that can make your clients appreciate why they can purchase from you unless the commodity you are selling falls within this group, which is also not a flagship product that varies every year. It would also help them grow faith in you as you will respond to any of their product queries without spending their time talking to anyone on the phone or heading to a shop to speak to somebody.

5.6   Are Confusing or Customizable:

Suppose an item is flexible or the option is unclear. In that case, the importance of offering advice and education about whether to do when, how to use a particular product, and how to configure it is just the same as above.

Again, you may quickly build an insightful platform if this thing is of a line that's not continuously shifting. It will make it even more challenging to create a knowledge center if the personalizations are continually evolving, but this is by no means unrealistic depending mostly on the product, particularly if the main part of the product stays the same, as it is the knowledge on the major pillar that would be more relevant than the customization options.

5.7   Require Installation or Setup:

This is maybe one of the simplest to choose: items that need to be technically assembled or set up, particularly when they're not simple. Let's presume you choose one and one website gave a device with a 2-page set-up manual while the other included a comprehensive guide which ran over many pages, including troubleshooting. Going back to the home protection system. What one will you purchase? The easiest approach to retain clients is to give the most knowledge and advice.

5.8   How to Add Value:

It is reasonably straightforward to contribute positively to the commodity and can be done in many ways:

✓ Build extensive buyer manuals

✓ Establish comprehensive lists and descriptions of goods

✓ Production of installation guides and details on setup

✓ Creating informative videos explaining how a given product functions

✓ Build a product reliability checklist or framework

5.9   Picking the Best Customers:

It is important to understand several demographic groups inside it, including after you have identified your target audience or consumer pool. You would like to be conscious of what markets the product would be involved in and how to better cater to the audience you would like to attract.

With the same umbrella, you should not lump both customers- you will notice that a consumer who orders a small, lower price item may want you would go to the moon and back with them. In contrast, a person buying anything pricier will actually ask you for anything other than the product they purchase.

You must attract the right market for your goods, and the three styles of consumers that follow appear to be the strongest to make the company worth running:

- **Hobbyists:**

Many persons have activities they truly want to do, and others invest large sums of money on machinery, instruments, and preparation. Bicycles that charge more than just a small car are driven by certain serious riders, whereas a keen fisherman invests a mind-boggling sum of money on tools. You would be offered a real leg-up in business by finding the correct hobbyist niche and being willing to provide them exactly what they want and need.

- **Businesses:**

Overall, company buyers can be a little more price-sensitive than Joe Blows, mostly on the corner, and they are going to buy in far greater amounts. Establishing a strong reputation and partnership with these corporations and gaining their confidence would enable you to build a long-term brand that sells in far greater amounts than individual consumers will purchase. Your best choice is to choose a commodity those appeals both to corporations and to customers.

- **Repeat Buyers:**

Whether you can find clients who renew the order, you are over to a positive thing since you have a steady source of sales. Selling disposable goods or products that need to be re-ordered often helps you expand your company easily and create what all organizations need: a loyal consumer base that returns to you time and time once more.

It may be nice to get all these consumers' styles, and none is always better than anyone. The main explanation that understanding where your consumer falls in is crucial is to ensure that you are able to react in the most productive way to their needs.

5.10 Other Considerations:

When you pick a commodity to market, there are a couple of other aspects that you must take into consideration:

- **Price:**

In regards to how you supply your clients with the pre-sales program, you must understand the price level. Some consumers are able to put an order digitally for $200 without first talking to anyone on the phone, but the buyers may not have been so willing if you are offering an item that costs $1,000. Some would prefer to speak to somebody about the goods first, not only about the products but also about making sure the job is done with a real shop.

You ought to be sure that you really are willing to provide effective phone service if you really are trying to market a high-priced commodity because that ensures that both you and your workers need to be informed regarding your product. To warrant the amount of funding, you will need to be sure that the profit margin is adequate. The sweet point for commodity costs often ranges between $50 and $200.

- **MAP Pricing:**

Manufacturers have set a Chart (minimum advertised price) for their individual goods, and all retailers would be required to sell at or beyond a certain amount. This avoids competitive pressures, which is a common dropshipping issue, and also ensures that decent profitability can be realized.

Look for vendors who implement MAP pricing, and the organization can reap income exponentially. It would just come back down to how good and persuasive the website and marketing plan is, with all rivals offering for the same amount, and you won't really have to think about getting pushed out of the competition by lower offers.

- **Marketing Potential:**

The entire scale of the demand for your goods is the revenue power of your company. You would like to make sure that you can bring the message out to more customers in the street as possible for your online store, and you will need to create a successful strategy to achieve this. A successful strategy, mostly by free channels, may contain ads.

It's too late to worry about ads day when you start your new company. This involves thinking about long in advance. In order to establish social networking accounts, publish posts, set up a blog and get active in discussions in your niche, website marketing seems to be the only way you can pull in new clients.

- **Plenty of Accessories:**

To make it more accessible, functional, or appealing, accessories are anything that can be applied to the product. It may be used to personalize and render a generic commodity more personal. It is a smart idea to have as many of them together in your online store as feasible if the commodity you want to offer comes well with the option of accessories. Customers want to be able to show their creativity and call their goods their own.

As a general guideline for shopping, the profits on high-priced goods are smaller than with the lower-priced accessories that go along with them. For starters, take the modest smartphone; most individuals can shop for the best deal because they're less inclined to do so when it comes to the system that goes with it. They're going to purchase it from the location they purchase their phone instead. It would have clients flocking in by being able to sell compatible products for big-ticket pieces. This is extremely true as you are willing to select accessories that any other stores do not sell. This is a case where it will be extraordinarily advantageous to have more than just one supplier for your online store.

- **Low Turnover:**

By now, you should be more inclined to make a sale if you can supply the goods with knowledge, guides, and education. Yet, if your preferred commodity is of a nature that varies every year, such as the mobile, it would be enormous the effort involved in having your site sustained. Stick on things that don't get modified continuously and keep the website running for even longer.

- **Hard to Find:**

If you can market a good that cannot be locally located too quickly, you have a greater chance of reaping the benefits. Do not be too particular here. They'd only head down towards their local hardware store if an individual needed to purchase a new home or garden fork. Selling anything a little more personal, though, such as falcon training tools, for instance, can pull about a certain amount of clients.

- **Small is the New Large:**

These days, several consumers expect free delivery, so if you want to deliver big-priced goods because you'll have to compensate for shipping, you would either lose sales otherwise you will lose buyers, and they won't be paying for shipping. It would be simpler for you to send out free or inexpensive by holding the goods thin.

It's not straightforward to choose the best niche, and you first have to take into account several different items. These are just the key criteria you need to follow when selecting your purchase.

The choices are infinite when it comes to identifying the product you would like to offer in your web shop, and it may be difficult to start shrinking down the choices in order to choose the item that will give you the best revenue and benefit. You will guarantee that you chose a commodity that will cater to the consumers who would be in the target demographic you are aiming to meet by considering and analyzing the product you choose to deliver. Knowing the future competitiveness of a commodity will inform you whether you have space in the sector and how you might easily wedge yourself in.

It will entail some time and effort to locate a valuable commodity. The devices and add-ons that would better suit it would also require some work of finding. If you discover this stuff, though, you will be able to put forth an entertaining e-commerce website and start turning a profit.

The next thing you're going to do is locate a source you can count on to get the goods you want in stock to send this out to your buyers in a timely fashion after identifying your position in the market and reaching a decision upon this product.

Chapter 6: The Blueprint:

It doesn't need to become a lengthy procedure to build up your virtual shop. Really, you will do so in a very short amount of time without being exhausted or lost if you recognize the measures to take and are mindful of certain do's and don'ts. This chapter explains precisely what details you have to know when you jump into the environment to operate an online company that requires vendors to sell their goods to your customers.

6.1   Selecting Your Product:

You have to decide what good you're going to offer in the store until you can start to build your shop.

- **Look For Product Ideas:**

There is no need to start a shop without a commodity to sell. Began with something you already need, or how you would fix your own problems or the difficulties people meet before you begin looking for fresh ideas about something you can sell. There are a small number of queries to be answered yourself:

- What are the goods or niches that concern you?

- What items are your mates excited about?

- What challenges do you have with your personal life? Whose goods can address this?

- What kind of corporations are there in your society? Can they be translated into a definition online? What corporations will cater to individuals beyond your culture in your society?

- In other areas of the planet, what goods are trending? In your culture, is there still a market for them? In your culture, will you build a market for them?

- If someone is unaware of the things, is there a relevant sector where you'd like to be tangled in? In that sector, what products are gaining popularity? What items can you consider useful in this industry?

- In other online retailers, what items are popular? Would you specialize in marketing this item? Is there really a specialty?

- What's the social curation website trend? Is there even an unexplored thing out there which individuals would want to see open to them?

6.2   Understanding Your Market:

Your target demographic is probably the most critical factor to remember (to whom one will sell there product). If you offer wedding stuff and dog toys both on the same platform, you're not supposed to be allowed to operate a profitable company. If someone is offering inexpensive t-shirts placed near expensive clothing, the same is real.

Consumers have thousands of goods and facilities in their hands. This suggests that there are boundless avenues in which you may reach the business. You have to find out who the target clients are so you can plunge straight in. Realizing who you deliver to would mean that you pick the best option for certain individuals. Any suggestions about how to identify your target group is given below.

Know, you will have various target audiences that could blend with the commodity you are trying to offer in various regions. Individually, with each target audience, take the following argument.

- **Select Explicit Demographics-Age:**

- This will be the purchaser's age, and whether they are diverse, the user's age.

- Gender-Like age can be the buyer's and user's gender.

- Marital Status.

- Ethnic Background.

- Occupation.

- Education Level.

- Income Level.

- **Consider The Psychographics:**

- Behavior

- Lifestyles

- Interests

- Values

- Attitudes

- Personality

- **Evaluate Your Choices:**

- Do you believe there are fairly broad communities of individuals that follow the criteria?

- Would the services help the target audience?

- Is your target group going to have a desire for the product?

- Do you grasp what drives choices to be created by your target audience?

- Would your target consumer be rich enough to afford your goods?

- Can your message hit them easily?

When selecting a commodity, some other tips:

- Know the contest

- Is the object anything you are comfortable with? if you are not Passionate about the commodity you would be offering, make sure that you become informative before you plunge into operating the company. Knowing the goods' pros and cons would mean that you'll have reliable customer support.

6.3   Choosing the Supplier:

One of the toughest choices you're going to be making as you set up your online shop is the provider you deal with. The provider with whom you collaborate has a huge effect on your company's performance, or you want to ensure that you chose the correct one.

There are a few items you have to do before you begin searching for that supplier:

- Ensure that you will show that you are a supplier. Have an EIN number for your organization and also a copy of your reselling certificate.

- Before you approach any possible vendors, be accustomed with dropshipping terms and also the typical dropshipping procedures.

You are able to go out to explore your provider until you are comfortable with dropshipping.

- **Know Your Industry:**

Various companies have various chains of supply. If you manage a small shop with a particular niche shop, you would be more effective if you work with a maker or a small regional supplier. You would be looking for a retailer with a wider range of goods they offer if you are trying to operate a larger shop of more products.

- **Try Industrialists First:**

If you figured out which one makes the goods you choose to sell, you would be talented enough to call the best way to find out if their things will be delivered. Although you may email them, contacting earning faster outcomes helps you get details quickly and even establish a business touch.

They can break into three groups when you contact multiple vendors:

- They Dropship-Great results for you, question their spouses about what one wants, and whether they have some minimum order conditions.

- Ask what vendors they sell their goods to; this will guide you on the right path to really be able to buy those products. They don't drop.

- At least people realize and are expecting to be ready to try somebody new. They don't sell their goods for resale.

- **Don't Depend On Search Engines To Catch Suppliers:**

Most vendors do not prioritize search engine optimization. This implies that you won't be able to discover them by conducting a Google search.

Use Trading Magazines – You can have vendors looking for you, but you will be able to find publications or updates targeted at your unique sector. There are also websites with previous problems in all of these magazines that will give you more support.

Forums And Online Groups – You will be able to find out what vendors other participants are using if you really can find a website or community that is unique to dropshipping and your business.

Conferences Or Trade Shows– You will be able to personally communicate with prospective vendors if you are eligible to join a trade show or meeting.

- **Other Options:**

Curated Lists: If you charge for viewing them, are open. Furthermore, any of the submissions might be incomplete or expired.

Using Google: Ascertain providers are not concerned about their web presence; this may be extremely time-consuming. Fast-forward to page ten or so and starting your quest there if you are trying to use Google to find.

6.4 Setting up the Web store:

It would be best to have the market aspects already worked out before you begin establishing your website. This involves your business's name, the items you will be offering and the prices for your items. The next items that you may require are:

- A web host

- A payment gateway

- A domain name and its extension

- A private SSL certificate

- A shopping cart script

- A dedicated IP address

You are happy to set up your website until you have the above stuff. Until it comes to configuring your website, you need two options. You may either build a home page as well as other static sites or use the shopping cart script as just a portal for your whole website (e.g., product background).

- **Building A Website:**

If you want to fully create a website despite utilizing the script for the shopping cart, it would require more time and effort. You would still have to provide a working knowledge of JavaScript, styling, and CSS. The next measures are, considering you have experience of these things:

Design: You need a simple understanding of how you want to build your web. That's before you begin off. The reality that your font options are minimal is one of the first items to know. Next, you'll have to know which pictures to be shown as photos as well as which backgrounds will be for one of your websites.

Preparation: For your concept, you will need to know the dimensions. This involves the column length and width, the spacing among them, and also the sum amount of both. You would basically need the measurements of a major part on the web. You're still going to require the simple issues, but not until long in the setup. First, utilizing HTML and CSS, you may need to build your web.

Deployment: You need to launch it once the website is configured and set up. Usually, this does not entail anything other than adding it to the webserver.

You can use the measures described here if you choose to use the shopping cart script as just a plugin for your site:

Installation: You would have to install the shopping cart device first. If you glance under your hosting tab's software/services segment, you will auto load the device. Based on the host and device you want to use, there might be several small variations, but they'll be identical.

You'll have to open up an archive folder while you update the device. This will decide where visitors will go as they reach your shop (such as directly to the product page, or an about page etc.)

Customization: Changing the emblem and deleting the footer graphic would be the first thing you can do. If you'd like to change it, you may also add a new subject or style to the payment gateway system. There'll be solutions in the shopping cart framework that might take care of both HTML and CSS for you, so you won't have to use any of the coding.

It's safer to use a shopping cart framework, but it still restricts the possibilities for establishing the website. When you recognize how to implement the source code to build the website you are designing for your company, the choices are almost infinite.

- **Setting Up The Ecommerce:**

If you are trying to process purchases via your web, a shopping cart framework of any kind is important. These will be the next measures after you've set up a shopping cart system:

- Get your bank's Internet retailer account-This will allow you to facilitate online credit card purchases.

- Get a Payment Gateway Account-This is an internet processor Shares credit card information from your client to your internet retailer account and authorizes credit card details

- Utilizing PayPal, which is an account-based method that is open to anybody with an email to easily transfer and collect cash with a credit card and bank account, is a less costly option to start receiving online payments.

6.5 Things to Keep In Mind While Conducting Business:

When you start on the road of launching an online company using the dropshipping model, there are some significant items you may want to hold in mind.

- Customer Satisfaction: Your client, even though you never see or talk to them, is a human. You want the consumer to be pleased because this is better achieved with great customer support. Place yourself in the shoes of your customer.

- Keep An Active Mailing List: Provide a discount for registering, such as free delivery, plus you will use their email account to submit newsletters regarding new product deals and promotions to attract your buyers coming back.

- Don't Oversell: Nobody needs to be under strain to purchase something. It's cool to point out the benefits of a product, but you wouldn't want to risk consumers when you point out a product's aspects too much.

- Keep Customer's Coming Back: Repeat tourists are a perfect way for the revenues to improve. It can bring your clients coming back by writing informative posts on the items you are offering, hosting transactions, and original material.

- Respond Quickly: It is essential to react as aspiring tourists to your site to give you messages or fill out their details for your address book. People can recall how long it would take you to reply to them and always enjoy a fast turnaround in reaction to a query.

Chapter 7: Getting Your Own Dropshipping Business off the Ground:

It is simpler than you imagine establishing your own dropshipping company, and it coincides with some wonderful benefits-not needing to react to someone but yourselves, reaping the benefits for the hard work you put into it and the freedom to pick where you operate from. Sadly, as they imagine launching their own company online, most people assume about one or two of these three things:

- I do not have the flexibility to operate a business.

- I do not have the resources to operate this operation.

- I don't have any expertise in operating an online business.

There is nothing else about these but apologies. You wouldn't need a lot of time—in fact, building up your online shop is perhaps the most time you invest. You can set up and completely run an e-commerce shop quicker than a day if you know how to use it.

Since you do not purchase any stock or have to incur costly overhead, you don't really need large sums of income. You need resources about the start-up, the website, its hosting domain name, etc., and you will find some decent discounts upon this if you search around.

Yeah, you might need a little bit in terms of experience, but it's not impossible to find by. Many hosting providers provide a bundle deal with a domain name and a website creator, along with complete guidance about doing it. You no longer need to become a computer engineer or coder, and you can also get the website for free through using Word Press if you pick items that you might create a blog about.

You have one thing in order to launch your new business:

7.1 A Web store:

Without getting a web store, you can't even sell goods online-this is the working aspect of the whole dropshipping method. The webstore seems to be the aspect that the clients see and where they buy their products; they couldn't see what was going on in the background, and they don't think much, though. A website should be simple to use for the clients and therefore should be visually attractive and inviting. The best way to create a website was about being professional in coding in years have gone by. There are other choices, but you can also create a website via coding and render it entirely your own. The method is all but automated nowadays. Those are the measures you ought to take to build a WordPress website (WordPress is one of the simplest to get begun with):

7.2 Get your domain name and a hosting package set up:

A domain name is how future users discover you and the blog you have focused on so hard. Each web server uses a Domain Name System to convert domain names into IP Addresses because the Internet is focused on IP addresses and not domain names. For your consumers, a strong domain name allows you far more available. For starters, in the www.WordPress.com URL, the domain name is "WordPress.com." The domain name's key part is "WordPress," and the extension is ".com."

Some modifications include: .com for companies, .org for businesses, .mobi for mobile device-only pages, .net is used for businesses and organizations, and .me will be used for private ventures. If you choose to use a U.S.-strictly related domain, .us is accessible, and .ca is accessible for Canadians.

Although you could get a low-level domain name and free hosting, these can create no lasting problems for you. Choosing the appropriate domain name and the proper hosting bundle is ideal for rating the search engines' website.

You ought to bear the aforementioned in mind regarding the domain name:

- To the company, the name must be appropriate.

- It is necessary to keep the name easy and brief.

- The name must have one that individuals would recall.

- The name should sound respectable.

The name must be available, with most hosting platforms testing the existence of domain names for you.

For a business, .com is the best extension for using. It's one of the more common extensions, and registration is often more costly for this purpose. If your company is promoted by word-of-mouth, though, it is more likely what individuals would be typed in if they recognize the name of your organization. A route around it is to choose a cheaper version such as .net to make it flow through your domain name in such a way that it has become part of your brand name, such as shopforyourpet.net. When your consumers say friends regarding your items, the rap and movement will enable your extension to be part of the brand.

Often, registering the organization for more than one extension is a smart idea. For example, if your site is awesomeshirts.com, you may suggest registering awesomeshirts.net and awesomeshirts.info as well so that by having almost the same domain name and another suffix, the competitor will not ride on your coattails. Though a domain name is not costly, it has never hurt to play safe, particularly as your company expands. If you're doing it, the domain may be bought and parked. This means the domain is all yours; however, no material on it prevents anyone else from accessing it. Unless the domain you chose seems to have a popularly misheard term in it, it is often a smart thing to do it, though.

You ought to pick a decent web host even if you have your domain name. Nothing other than a signpost, the domain name guides visitors to the directory that houses the website. This server should be able to drive what your website requires and the manner you want it to be operated. This has been the most costly aspect of launching your own dropshipping firm, but you don't have to invest a lot, check around and buy some better offers, but use these parameters to do so:

- However, search customer feedback aims to rate platforms that are separate from the host you are taking into consideration.

- Make sure that the host will run WordPress

- Confirm that cPanel, DirectAdmin or any other such related host is operating device as the rear end of them. What this indicates is that with only a single key, you would be able to install WordPress.

- Test their customer support. User feedback will inform you what you are doing. It's just necessary to recognize

- Please ensure that the country or countries that you will have fast servers Webstore goals.

In the next stage you'll have a domain name and a successful hosting plan set up:

7.3   Install Word Press:

WordPress is perhaps the simplest tool for creating a website, avoiding all the scripting and enabling you to focus on the website's content. WordPress is a prominent platform used by a wide spectrum of entities, including writers, news agencies, Fortune 500 firms, and even stars. WordPress is free and will be used from a platform to a registry to manage just about every site, and often a discount site, a work board, a booking system, a help desk, a location for classified advertising, and an online shop, of the subject. You would be able to develop your app on top of its current APIs and built-in user protection and management features by opting to use WordPress as a platform. This will enable you to create a unique and simple website to set up and simple to use by your clients. As I said before, your host should be run cPanel or DirectAdmin; the most popular and simplest to use is cPanel. Part of the explanation why cPanel is more prevalent is that it groups the functionality into sections, making it easy to explore unique features. CPanel also offers many more features and extensions than DirectAdmin, which allows you more options for setting up your website. You can get an email once you sign up with your host, providing you complete guidance about setup WordPress-for DirectAdmin;

you will have to click on the "Installation Applications Installer" page, while in cPanel, the "Install WordPress in 1 Click" link will tell. Tap on them and obey the on-screen directions for a quick download of WordPress.

7.4 Installing and Configuring WordPress Themes:

One of WordPress's greatest components is that you might configure what is essentially a very simple structure to suit your requirements. You have to pick a theme and activate it to make the website appear nice and cater to prospective clients. A theme would be nothing just over a design that is scribbled over the upper edge of WordPress, and a broad range of different ones can be found, a few free, some are not.

Although there are thousands of theme choices, you do not really want to press on the first one you find that you like and think is going to fit with your business. Before reaching a definitive judgment about the style you would use, you can remember some other aspects.

- Simplicity – You cannot need a theme of loads of colors, intricate templates, and dazzling animations. While this would be useful for certain pages, goods should be held clean and tidy for a platform that is attempting to market and encourage the items to become the star of the website, not the backdrop.

- Responsiveness – A sensitive theme is one that adapts the style to varying sizes and gadgets of the display. Because a lot of website traffic is produced from smartphones and other handheld devices, a theme that would respond appropriately is a massive benefit and will create navigation easier for your customers. You can risk losing consumers to certain other web stores with reactivity if your theme is not sensitive.

The style you choose can either apply or, at minimum, not be contrary to the item you are trying to market. For starters, if you're attempting to sell snowshoes, never use a beach theme, while a theme that's all blues with greens will be ideal for selling some items.

You should pick your style and maybe go ahead and tailor that to your specific needs. To create your theme genuinely personalized to you, here are a few key items you'll really want to change:

- The logo – Changing the branding of your own

- General settings – This would be where if you want to use Google Analytics, you can insert in the monitoring code you would be given.

- Side panels and sliders – If your theme does have side panels and sliders, you may have to Set them up to include any material in them,

- Subscribe and Connect module – This would be where your clients would be Subscribe to your mailing list and your accounts on social media.

Your theme is now designed to appear fantastic and tempt future clients to try both the platform and the items you advertise.

7.5   Install an e-commerce Plugin:

Webstore functionality is not included in WordPress, but plugins are permitted. Find a decent e-commerce plugin-Woo Commerce is among the strongest and simplest, but you'll need a friendly theme and enable it and trigger it.

Your plugin would need to be equipped with specific statistics, such as currencies, shipping costs, respectively. Install anything that significantly changes, but charge particular attention to the following:

- **Pages:**

To lead your consumers to the data they are searching for, your website's links are essential. You would want eight pages to guarantee that your website facilitates optimum consumer navigation.

- Welcome: The welcoming page is being used to invite customers to your shop and display as an overview some relevant or helpful details that you think the consumer should receive.

- About Us: The about us tab is being used to include the details they would like to know to prospective clients to persuade them to opt to buy with you rather than anyone else. This page must be informative and likable. It's not enough to suggest that you are the strongest about what you offer; you have to show it.

- Contact Us: The Contact Us section is being used to offer choices for clients of how to reach you to provide input or pose questions. This page will have a feedback form, which can be filled out along with an email address if, rather than filling out a form, they want to communicate through their email account. If you have contact info, it is often beneficial to use it and the hrs. on this page to contact you.

- New Product: A future product page would enable your clients to see the new items you are selling to attract repeat sales. Only to see what innovative products you are selling can customers come to your website.

- Top Products: The top items are bought by consumers more commonly. On this list, you would like to position items that are often the most likely to cater to potential clients that have high ratings that would inspire clients to come to store and spend more.

- Promotions: Using to let clients aware about any deals that you are providing.

- Privacy Policy: It is a legal document that advises your clients how to use the confidential details they supply the organization with.

- Terms and Conditions: This is being used to control the clients' interaction with you; it is a civil contract. Payment rates, delivery terms, and all other significant detail would be covered.

You may also opt to include some custom widget pages that you consider align for your webstore, like details pages or news articles that might apply to your goods, and improve user usability.

Be sure that all of the sites are appropriately installed, whether some are missed or whether they will not function properly.

- **Taxes:**

This would rely on the country of birth, but most need you to render it very simple if any taxes are added. Ensuring the plugin is installed at the checkout to display the taxes.

- **Payment Settings:**

When you start having clients, it's fantastic, but if you wouldn't offer them money to charge, it's all pointless. This happens in situations where you take the money on the dropshipped goods. This is not important where the retailer handles the transaction.

- **Shipping:**

You ought to let the buyers exactly how much it will pay for delivery they should expect. Although if you may not push these expenses through to the clients, to guarantee that the consumer is not paying more or less than clients should be, you will need to customize the settings correctly. It also encourages clients to be mindful of the payments they may receive until the purchase is finished.

7.6 Populate Your Products:

You must have a website address, a hosting kit and a completely functional website for WordPress by now. It's ready now to put any merchandise to sell. The next logical move is to pick your vendors, and further, I may get to that. You actually need to know how to integrate it for the objectives of this.

Be sure that the title of the product is straightforward, not too lengthy and simple to comprehend. Any information of the commodity must be contained. First, you must ensure that your product's definition is straightforward, comprehensive and simple to comprehend. Be sure that the types of goods are clearly defined, and so are the type of commodity, type of delivery, price, article code, and any other details that the consumer wants to see.

An effective approach to stop frustrating your clients is to break your goods into divisions. You want to make sure that each page in the category is clearing, well-structured and does not confuse your clients. It should be published repeatedly if a commodity falls into more than one group, so the user can quickly locate it irrespective of where they search.

It is also important to add images-most individuals would not purchase after knowing what the result exists like. The illustration that your referred vendors use will be used. Be sure that you don't use so many videos because people prefer to skip and don't enjoy the visual variety if there are many more to look at. It is crucial, though, to fully explain the product, as clients are more inclined to recall a product presented to them orally. Make sure you teach the consumer how and when to use goods and whether they want to purchase them.

You have indeed selected and enrolled a domain name and plugin that will direct clients to your webstore efficiently. With a clear and welcoming style, you have really been able to build your shop effectively, and the sites are designed out in a user-friendly manner and helps your clients navigate what they're searching for without becoming overwhelmed.

That's really all it truly takes up a decent e-commerce shop for your drop ship items to be sold. We will focus on how to pick the best items in the next part.

Chapter 8: The Risks and Drawbacks:

During the first 12 months of trade, nearly 50 percent of all startup firms are doomed to collapse; however, there are avenues you might stop being one of those figures. In order to secure that you will not become another company that has attempted and struggled, several measures should be accomplished. You would be able to stop slipping into all of those pits and become more likely to excel if you can recognize what contributes to most enterprises to collapse.

By proper preparation, the first approach to eliminate loss is. You're bound through some difficult times, and it's surely not going to be smooth sailing. This occurs in both existing and emerging enterprises. You would be continually struggling with one issue or another, regardless of how deep you are in the company; the first year is excellent preparation for the remainder of the period you are supposed to be in business. It would surely allow you to find the best way through the challenges by making a clear strategy and pursuing it in the correct direction. Your organization could rise as a leading candidate if you're doing it correctly, stronger than you might ever have expected. You should be conscious of the issues confronting most startup businesses that eventually leave them in a lengthy list of failed companies to build a strategy that can successfully hold you in the company. You ought to work out how you will escape the very things endured by many other firms from collapsing.

8.1 Risks:

You should be completely informed of the risks associated until you start the dropshipping business:

- **Supplier Reliance:**

You are always relying on certain vendors, no matter how often you obey all the manuals, all the guidelines, and sourcing your goods from many different providers. They are also the ones who will have the stock because they're the ones who, within the timeframe you negotiate with your consumers, ship it out to your consumers.

It is pretty much out of your reach after the order is being moved on to the retailer. There's not much you could do to manage how things proceed from there until.

Much of the time, things can run well, but you are the one who meets an angry consumer when everything goes wrong; a buyer who may do your name some significant hurt. It would help if you had a strategy in motion to be prepared to cope with disgruntled consumers on the occasional event that your provider encounters a challenge and cannot reach the quality your customers want. By already getting a strategy in motion to reward a disgruntled consumer before they can have an opportunity to distribute some bad feedback regarding your company, you will guarantee that you please the customer, and therefore, the client will turn their attention to the positive customer support they got. Don't intend to accuse the retailer solely. Most clients will never recognize this as a good reason for the mistake. It is you they value to ensure that they get their Paid-for object. Trying to blame your provider would render you dishonest and look like a cop-out. The right way to do this would be to apologize for the mistake and provide a method of repairing it.

- **Using Many Resources:**

In order to guarantee that you would procure the goods until you need them, you must have arrangements with a variety of suppliers. Even so, you cannot fall into the pit of displaying every product on your website from every single supplier. You face the risk of a client buying many pieces, each from a separate source if you're doing it, and that makes it complicated and expensive.

For and particular supplier, one choice is to get a separate browser and, as you launch out, aim to adhere to only one vendor to start with setting up a website does cause expenses, and you want to hold them down before you are developed. On a single platform, it is possible to provide more than one provider and encourage your clients to buy from any of them. This ensures, though, that you'll have to be mindful of stock quantities, and you may have to buy and transfer and manage the excess costs individually so that the shipments can be met. A simple approach to do it is to restrict the additional stock offerings to the key product apparel that are not likely to charge you a tone of extra shipping cash. Often, aim to restrict it to goods from which you can earn enough cash to pay the delivery. If you would like to use more than one distributor right from the outset, another choice is to continue to use vendors who offer the same goods because if and when appropriate, you can have one as a replacement. If the commodity is extremely common and sometimes runs out of storage, one explanation you can need a substitute supplier is.

- **Order Tracking:**

In order to send your shipments, you are entirely dependent on your distributor, and you would find it challenging, if not unlikely, to maintain track of the goods when your provider is shipping them. This might trigger problems because your company won't appear trustworthy, and your consumer can't monitor their order. In reality, since order monitoring is now a common part of any purchase, and there's every chance of your clients challenging the whole order. When there is a busy period of the year, such as Christmas, this sort of problem will trigger far more difficulties, since this is where more packages are lost than will usually happen.

There are a few multiple ways that you can tackle this problem. One choice is to do all the delivery with your account for consumers. This suggests that it must be the retailer's duty to prepare the order and call the delivery agent for which you share an acct and then have the item delivered to your client. This will allow you to gain tracking for any order processed and delivered by you. Although there are benefits to this, it is a time-consuming approach that may seem to beat the aim of using dropshipping to manage the business.

Things have progressed a little further in recent times because digital software programs could be used by the couriers and vendors to share distribution details. Despite signing up, before you approach a retailer, inquire whether they have a mechanism in place to track orders. If there is indeed a mechanism to manage shipments, that can make the delivery phase even simpler for the customers. If a method to monitor the orders is not in operation, inquire if that's something, the retailer aims to introduce in the immediate future.

8.2   Differences in Products:

You are most likely to concentrate on introducing new items and developing your connections while establishing up your new company and focusing on your social networking page. It does not happen to you that the retailer or seller may have modified or even withdrawn the items you have put on your website. While concentrating on expanding your connections is vital, it is also essential to ensure that the product range is updated and open to your consumers.

You would have to go back to the customer to clarify that they will not be allowed to get the commodity they assumed was accessible if you wind up offering an item to your client that you do not deliver. This will make you feel like a bit of a fool and very humiliated, and when consumers receive differentiated products, or they don't obtain their shipment at all, it will do significant harm to your credibility. The latest iteration of a product might be improved but might be more costly, and a lack of attention ensures that it is up to you to pay the added burden, not your client. It could also not achieve something that, in the first instance, the client needed it for. It is worth defending yourself a disgruntled client, not to mention the financial you can waste due to the mistake, to take a little time checking that the deals are still current.

A piece of data like this is really simple to lose, and it can have significant implications for the business. Ensure you chose one that gives constant updates on their goods unless you choose a supplier, particularly if they are updated or withdrawn. You will definitely do something now on your page if they tell you. Getting them to inform you about product updates would also save you the period to regularly review each product.

If you do not locate a seller that can give feedback about their goods, suggest making the product range limited enough that you have the opportunity to periodically keep a close eye on the goods or opt to market a separate product portfolio.

- **Failing to Plan Properly or Not at All:**

This should be rational thinking that very careful preparation is the best way to organize a profitable enterprise. The more comprehensive your strategy is, the more well thought out it is, the simpler it is to cope with circumstances and concerns. There are, therefore, two key challenges related to the preparation that may place the company at very severe risk of failure:

- A failure to prepare implies that you do not attempt to consider what challenges you will encounter, which hurdles can obstruct your path, or even find the right way to start. That still doesn't mean immediate failure; it also implies that it would be far more challenging to attain progress.

- Over preparation is as poor as not training at all. One side of the coin means you're going to waste too much preparing; you're not going to have the opportunity to swap. You would be so concentrated on continuing to prepare that the real company gets moving for any possible scenario. You can't do this because just because it hasn't yet begun, the company will collapse. The other side of the coin suggests you're going to make a strategy and you're going to start the company, but you stick so closely to the plans that you don't have to contend with things now when anything occurs was not prepared for. This suggests that versatility falls out from the window, and it loses profits.

There have been some pretty severe dangers, and also the dangers of dropshipping, which can throw the company totally off balance right at the moment when you sound like things have gone well. If you incorporate them throughout your schedule and are organized, most, maybe not all, of these could be avoided:

- **Competition:**

For developers, the low costs associated with launching a dropshipping company render it a simple option. For this precise cause, though, several individuals want to establish their own dropship companies, and rivalry is harsh. The competition can become crowded in certain niches to the extent where you can hardly make a profit. While holding the rates down to draw clients is crucial, you do not have to offer the lowest possible price on the market.

Building up your brand and getting recognized for having little more than a commodity is the only way to get around this. You want clients to recognize that you provide the highest level of customer support and aftercare purchases, and experience of the items you market. You may also try providing a nice delivery bundle to ensure the clients have their orders shipped sooner or get a free product that would encourage them to come back to you.

A strong return strategy is yet another perfect means of having an advantage over a rival. Cost is not the guiding force besides a client selecting a firm. Customers expect a business they can believe and count on to provide them with the finest of all at all times. Customers still like to ensure that if they accidentally wind up with a substandard product or an item that is not what they were anticipating, you would cover them. And if you charge a bit higher than your rivals, if they believe your organization is legitimately stronger than your rivals, clients will pay it.

- **Logistics:**

It is necessary to have various websites going, several different vendors and loads of different items to make a decent living and operate a profitable dropshipping company. You would, though, have strong logistical help to do all that. You have to ensure sure the machine handles all your shipments on schedule enough so your vendors can perform their job full time.

Automating all the devices is the perfect way to do this. An effective system would make ensuring that the requests from the clients are delivered to the correct supplier. Successful software would be able to monitor the item for you in the world where technology has advanced and alert you if anything has gone wrong in an order. Until your consumer realizes that there may be an issue, you will reach your client with a suggestion rather than your client coming to you with a problem you weren't expecting.

Having failed to do this will ensure requests are skipped or incorrect details are given to the retailer, ensuring the consumer picks the wrong product. The risks involved in monitoring and handling orders, particularly when you have quite a variety of orders from various places and with different vendors, can get difficult quite quickly and can end up leaving a lot of time to figure out. This prohibits you from becoming able to propel the organization further to boost your image and your earnings.

Do not believe that you will handle the operation of several web stores without any sort of integrated framework. While having to manage several shops manually, the only goal you can do is to stress oneself out and potentially wind up without any firms because of mix-ups and misunderstanding.

- **Too Much Time on Social Media:**

You may still spend too much time on your social networking accounts in almost the same way that you really can spend a lot of time on the company's logistical side. This will be so convenient to do when you would be speaking to people most of the time. It is nice to be accessible on social networks to address queries from your client that would inspire more customers to buy from you. This may quickly go to the point that it ceases supporting the organization and hinders it.

It can seem an insane concept that so much time engaging with your clients might cause problems with your company, but it does occur. This is because you will not spend that much time with most of your company while you are wasting all the time reacting on social media. Some of the market elements that often need your time involve checking that the retailer accepts client requests and that the goods you have on the platform are still current. If this is your drawback, you'll have to cut down on your company's aspects that need it to deal with much more critical problems and start wasting time on them. Get a plan and conform as tightly as possible to it.

- **A Means to an End:**

Too many individuals start a dropshipping company and see that as the only thing; their dreams do not require continuing on from the initial company. In fact, dropshipping is an excellent place to boost a low-overhead and low-risk enterprise, but as it develops, it can only be part of a longer-term strategy involving both dropshipping and keeping upon your own inventory.

If you only commit to dropshipping for the long run, you rely on your vendors and the economy forever, and if conditions shift, you just don't have the space to switch with them. When your provider goes out of service, what occurs? You ought to prepare for your dropshipping company to be only a component of a larger business and get to a stage where you have a reasonable degree of influence over the business and less chance of losing all this in a moment.

- **Product Descriptions:**

The first is to import a product summary straight from the retailer or distributor's copy, and the next is to adhere to brief reviews, and then you'll have more goods displayed on the website. There are two items that several drop-shippers fell afoul of. Next, since the web pages can dramatically reduce the scores, lengthy explanations that have been replicated, word for word, by the retailer or producer can bring you nowhere quickly. You would like to guarantee that anything you post to your web is clear of copyright infringement and exclusive to your site to optimize your web search scores. There are choices for requesting or recruiting someone to perform your company's writing part for you if you are not professional in writing. You might also notice that the client may only go to your provider by taking you out of the loop.

Second, brief explanations won't provide enough detail to the consumers to base their buying decisions on. Using the definition of the maker as a reference instead, then revise the description. Make sure to hold things as comprehensive as practicable. Get a preview of the items, maybe you can, or buy one for you to make sure that anything about the summary is correct and does not leave any questions for the buyer. When you prepare your product information, another point to bear in mind is to bring them understandable. If all of the text is compressed into one paragraph, bullets and line spacing are your mates; it would be impossible for the customer to understand.

Place yourself in your buyers' shoes and consider whether, if you were dreaming of purchasing one of your items, you'd like to see. Use your terms, including the data in your explanations, and maximize your explanation's usefulness.

- **Check out a Dropshipper:**

Please ensure you search them out thoroughly before you sign the papers with every retailer to manage your orders and distribute your packages. Verify how long they have really been selling, if they're not credible, and read feedback from independent consumers. Ensure that the provider you are utilizing is approved to resell their goods by the producer and that they cannot give the consumers a rip-off edition of the item.

Another point you need to do is ensure they're really manufacturers rather than drop shippers. The logistics would become a true nightmare if you wanted to put your orders into another drop shipper. Along with getting little leverage over the cost of the goods, you would not really be willing to compete in terms of the price you sell your clients. All you can actually do is apply an added expense to the item, and since the item will be inexpensive somewhere, your consumers would possibly wind up disobeying your business entirely. Asking about a specific address or a domain name is a reasonable way to ensure you do not use another dropshipping business. When it takes you to a shop that appears like yours, it's not a retailer.

Keep your eyes open and first-order those research items. This would inform you what their client experience is like and what speed they are running at. That's the most significant aspect of the method, maybe, and you can't hurry it. It should not be emphasized sufficiently because the provider you want to offer your consumer dropship goods is an essential aspect of your organization and you need to make sure you choose somebody who can improve your company and not cause new issues for you.

- **Stock Levels and Back Order Systems:**

They should have an inventory chain that you can link to guarantee availability levels, no matter which vendors you want to deal with. This would guarantee that the website is still up-to-date and that inventory levels and usability are still accurate. This ensures that you won't have to inform your clients that they will wait on their product and it's not in storage. The last move you want to be doing at the same stage is to start putting back-order requests. When it happens to a back-ordered product, there are just two choices, and none of them is perfect for you as well as your client.

One solution is to keep the buyer's payment and inform them that you would have the item for them when it has become in stock. This is dangerous as rules prohibit you from holding the client's money for a certain period. If the clock runs at around the same rate as the commodity becomes in inventory, the expense of a purchase that the buyer subsequently gets will be refunded. Another choice is to refund the buyer's money and inform them whenever the commodity is available to order and assume they will like it.

Not only can you face the transaction's failure, but it is also a disaster with the logistics concerned, and you can have to cope with it. As they prepare for an order that you've no influence about and might well have neglected, the consequence could well be the failure of a business. This is the best way, not something you would like to do, to hurt your credibility. That's why it is really important to keep the product listings updated.

Operating an online store that certainly utilizes drop shipping is not without its threats and obstacles. It is utterly vital to the future to be equipped for the difficulties of operating as a middle guy between the client and the seller.

It is crucial to recognize all the factors that may theoretically trigger you to lose cash and clients to be prepared, effectively shutting down your company. These problems are evident, such as goods going out of inventory, rip-offs, and delayed packages. Some others are less apparent but also just as essential to your company's success, such as investing so much time on social media and not spending lots of time on your product details.

Make sure you search the supplier out, hold the contact lines open with them, and not be scared to ask those queries. They would like you to choose them, basically, and they'll be able to address every query that you have to persuade you to use them above any other provider. If you have recognized all the possible drawbacks and threats that can impact the business, until they become a crippling concern, you will be able to make a strategy to prevent them.

Conclusion:

While drop shipping will offer you the ideal opportunities to begin a company, particularly if you have little financial and expertise along the way, it cannot be seen as an easy scheme to really get rich. You ought to treat it like you would any market opportunity, with integrity, to be effective. Yom needs a solid strategy, and you certainly have to decide on realistic targets. Sometimes, it may be easier to break it into a set of smaller targets if you have one primary objective, which you can accomplish weekly or monthly. This is important whether you are to see if the company is going to be very successful or not. Likewise, if you notice that you're not just hitting the location you need to be in, you should revise your status and all the choices in accordance with the strategy and how the company is going. Whenever appropriate, you may also make adjustments to your schedule.

Perhaps one of the most dynamic of all market models is dropshipping. It can be challenging to select the right segment and the right goods without running up against strong competition from companies that have already been founded. You ought to decide the right way to do this if you are in this situation but may not want to improve your niche or market segments. There might be items you may sell that cannot be offered to consumers by your leading rivals.

By checking at the platforms on which it is involved, where it brings the biggest out of it, and what strategies it employs in terms of promotion, you will learn a lot about your opponent. This can teach you how you can better deliver something new than what they are doing, something that adds importance to your clients. Research your competitors hard and see what they do well and what they're doing wrong. If a consumer feels they have more money from you, they're going to buy from you; then you can potentially poach consumers very quickly in this manner.

Dropshipping can provide a fantastic way to start a company at low cost, but smaller profit margins can come at a premium. If you are trying to be competitive for only a dropshipping organization, you would need to have a very large amount of clients purchasing or a large product range buying each commodity from consumers. To create awareness, you can use social networks to advertise your goods and their messaging strategy if you're using them to advertise your goods. Traditional advertisement with a dropshipping the company often operates really well.

I have volunteered to convince you to develop a deeper understanding of dropshipping and what it entails with this book; how someone can start a dropshipping company. How you communicate with individuals and the quality of customer support you deliver is the true secret to success. That's what can set you apart in your niche from everybody else.

Being conscious of bogus vendors and scams is one crucial factor you could remember. Newcomers to the dropshipping market will quickly fall victim to fraudsters, and if they're not doing the right homework, they will fast and always lose a lot of money. Stand back as they are most likely false and after nothing other than your income if dropshipping supplier requests for cash upfront or even monthly.

There'll be some scammers for any legitimate company out there; however, as you must know now, the actual costs of beginning a business are tiny. The expenditures of putting up your website and managing it are what you pay for. When it is purchased, all the stock is accounted for, not afterward, and it is when the client makes an order with you.

Maintaining clear communication lines, staying in touch with your clients and establishing close relationships is the very best way to make sure that your drop shipping company is effective. If they want to come back and if they want to say someone about you, they have to believe you. Please ensure your consumer contact informs them of what you're doing for them, how much you can give in terms of pricing, and this would guarantee that your brand remains squarely in their imaginations.

If you have a strong partnership with them, you can find it simpler to cope with any complications, such as lost or wrong orders, and you must still retain contact with your vendors. The ability to special pricing deals, decent prices, or first call on stock can even be provided to you when availability is restricted.

For reading my novel, I would really like to thank you. I think it has provided you with the motivation you want to see that you could start a company with little capital, and you'll be a great drop shipper. There are still lucrative niches open to you, but there are still goods that will earn you a decent return, in spite of the strong rivalry you will encounter. Make sure to learn your niche well and appreciate your business. Although dropshipping doesn't open you up to many of the dangers of conventional e-commerce firms, it can also break apart and cost you cash.

You will come up with a good company with a bit of work and a lot of wits and use that as a starting stone for the future.